FYSON, N.L.
Growing up in the 1970s

TO5184

St. Benedict

St. n

HEALEY, TIM

THE 1970S

942.086 .

TO5184

J. Johnson

20.12.91 (Mr G.)
office.

10T.

Growing up in
THE 1970s

Nance Lui Fyson

B.T. Batsford Ltd   London

Typeset by Tek-Art Ltd, Kent
and printed in Great Britain by
R J Acford
Chichester, Sussex
for the publishers
B.T. Batsford Ltd,
4 Fitzhardinge Street
London W1H 0AH

ISBN 0 7134 5109 2

Frontispiece: **"The Muppet Show" and "World
Champ" were two of many popular T-shirts.**

Acknowledgments

The Author and Publishers thank the following for
their kind permission to reproduce copyright
illustrations: British Home Stores, frontispiece,
figures 48, 49; Manpower Service Commission,
figure 15; The Photo Source, figures 1, 2, 3, 4, 5, 6,
7, 8, 9, 10, 11, 12, 13, 14, 16, 17, 18, 19, 20, 21, 22, 23,
24, 25, 26, 27, 28, 29, 30, 31, 32, 33, 34, 35, 36, 37,
38, 39, 40, 41, 42, 43, 44, 45, 46, 47, 50, 51, 52, 53,
54, 55, 56, 57, 58, 59, 60. The photographs on page
70 were taken by Nance Lui Fyson.

The Author would also like to thank the following
for their help: The Council for Educational
Technology; The Grocer Magazine; Hamley's Toys;
Music Week; Toys International Magazine; Lillian
Simmons; William Broderick.

Contents

The Illustrations

1 The 1970s

Children in the 1970s were busy as ever copying the adult world. In 1972 one *seven-year-old* boy in Scotland had his first date. A newspaper reported how he took his girlfriend, "a dishy little blonde, also seven" out to dinner. He wore his best Highland rig-out. She had a special hair-do, navy dress, red shoes and handbag. The 87p bill was paid by the boy from his pocket money. They had chicken, chips, ice cream and Coca-Cola. The boy remarked: "We are just good friends, but I wanted to take her out somewhere nice." The girl said shyly: "It was lovely."

New age of majority
The decade opened formally recognizing young people as "grown-up" at an earlier age. The Family Law Reform Act lowered the age of majority from 21 to 18 as of 1 January 1970.

Eighteen-year-olds were allowed the rights to sell houses, make wills, go to law, apply for passports, marry without consent and buy on hire purchase without a guarantor. Andy Alexander (b. 1960) living in London: "Kids were growing up a lot faster. That's a sad fact of life.".

Children's Rights
The 1970s was a decade of protest and of demanding rights and equality. Groups of every kind, including such minorities as homosexuals, were asking openly for fairer treatment. Children, too, were making their voices heard. In 1970 the National Council for Civil Liberties launched a campaign to give children more say in decisions affecting them. *Children's Rights* was published in 1971, both as a book and as a new magazine. The National Union of School Students was set up in 1972 to help pupils have more say in the way schools were run. It launched a "school students' charter" calling for no corporal punishment, no school uniform, no petty rules, no prefects, no secret files. By 1976 there were 15,000 members paying 10p each a year. A 1978 survey found a growing number of local education authorities accepting pupil involvement in school government. The new

1   A keen space fan wore his toy spacesuit to the new Liverpool Museum planetarium in 1970. Space travel was a growing interest for many young people. The Americans first put a man on the moon in 1969, and landed the first manned vehicle in 1971.

Education Act 1980 actually empowered L.E.A.s to appoint pupil governors over age 16.

The Electronics Revolution

Changes in technology had an impact on many areas of life. The very earliest computers were large machines. The invention of transistors began a revolution in the early 1950s. By the early 1960s, somewhat smaller computers were in use. Later, the silicon chip allowed integrated circuits to perform the job of hundreds of transistors. Such "chips" became the basis of microcomputers appearing in the Seventies.

The rate of changes in electronics over the 1970s was startling. Electronic watches first appeared in 1967 and the market for them grew steadily from 1971. John Alexander (b. 1958), who was at school near Oxford, first

2 Sir Clive Sinclair launched the world's first pocket TV set in 1977. Sinclair became a household name in the 1970s. In 1972 he brought out the world's first pocket calculator (which sold for £79), in 1974 the matchbox radio and one of the first digital watches in 1975. In 1980 there was ZX 80, the first home computer selling for under £100.

saw one in a James Bond film. "I thought, 'That's for me.' Real snazzy." By 1978 nearly 40% of all watches sold were of the digital type. The pocket calculator, introduced in the early 1970s, was another example of electronic changes. Prices of these fell rapidly over the decade, making such items available to a wide public – children and teenagers as well.

General Elections

The 1970s was also a time of changing governments and party leaders. Conservative Edward Heath became Prime Minister in 1970. Labour's Harold Wilson replaced Heath after the General Election of February 1974. This new Parliament was the shortest since 1886. The country went to the polls again in October 1974 and Wilson was re-elected. Jane Elton (b. 1964) remembers a mock election at her school near Southampton: "I was the Liberal candidate. Our results showed the Conservatives winning, but in the real election Labour won." Margaret Thatcher was chosen as the new leader for the Conservative Party in 1975. As the first woman party leader in Britain, she led the Conservatives to victory in May 1979.

Re-named counties

Even the map of Britain changed in this decade. Some people found themselves in a re-named county. The Local Government Act 1972 re-organized local government in England (outside Greater London) and Wales. From 1 April 1974, Cumberland, Westmorland and the Furness area of Lancashire became the re-named single county of "Cumbria". Rutland disappeared as a separate county, being merged with Leicestershire. Three completely new counties formed were Avon, Cleveland and Humberside. There were other changes as well.

Population changes

The population of over 55 million in Britain in 1971 was 2½ million more than in 1961. The number then grew only very slowly during the 1970s. The overall increase from 1971 to 1981 (with England up 0.4%, Wales up 2.2% and Scotland down 2.1%) was considerably less than the population rises of about 5% in both the 1950s and 1960s.

Children were somewhat less likely to be living in London and other big cities by the end of the decade. London's population fell by 10% over the 1970s, to below 7 million people for the first time since 1901.

Decimal coinage

A big money change in the early 1970s was the start of decimal coinage. "D-Day" was 15 February 1971. Heather McNeil (b. 1965), who lived near Glasgow: "On the day, me and my mum went shopping. In the bakers, the lady showed us them all, what the new coins were going to look like."

The Decimal Currency Board had been preparing the country for months before, explaining how the new money would help bring Britain into line with Europe. Children in 1970 were used to handling pounds, shillings (20 of those to one pound) and old pence (12 of those to one shilling). All this old money was in circulation along with the new decimal pounds and pence until the end of August. Price signs gradually no longer showed numbers like 7/6 (7 shillings and 6 old pence) or 6d (6 old pence). In 1977 a new, slightly smaller one-pound note was introduced.

VAT

Another money change in the early 1970s was the start of VAT (Value Added Tax) in 1972. This added 8% to the cost of some goods and services. VAT was levied on children's clothes over the size of "an average 13-year-old". This meant extra costs for the parents of large children. When the VAT rate was raised in 1977, clothes for a big 11-year-old were costing 15% more than clothes for a small 14-year-old. Parents involved MPs in their protests and campaigns.

High inflation

Rapid price rises were a fact of 1970s life. In June 1975 inflation was at a staggering 36%. In the early 1970s the government tried freezes on pay and prices, but high inflation continued. Even children noticed prices going up. A small bag of crisps cost 7d in 1970 (equal to just over 2½p). By 1979 the bag was costing 8p.

Crime and vandalism

Recorded crime in England and Wales went up

3 Damage on a British Rail train caused by soccer fans, 1973. By 1978, vandalism was costing BR £3-5 million per year and London Transport £1 million. Local authorities were facing vandalism bills of £3 million a year for housing estates and £15 million for school buildings. Deliberate damage to telephone boxes was costing the GPO £1 million.

by 50% over the years 1973-77. Burglaries especially became more common. By 1977 there were nearly 12,000 burglaries every week, equal to 70 every hour. Many children found their own home disrupted.

The increasing crime of the Seventies included crime by young people. Those aged 14-16 had the highest rate of reported offences of *any* age group. Andy Alexander (b. 1960), living in London: "When I was 13, 14, breaking into parking meters was the big thing. The meters used to be easy. Smash smash smash with a sledge hammer and they would crack. Or another way was to remove the lock. They used to have a very simple lock."

The number of girls in trouble with the police was much lower than the number of boys. However, in England and Wales, girls aged 14-16 in the 1970s were *6 times* more likely to be found guilty or cautioned for some indictable offence than girls in the late 1950s. (For boys in the same age group, the figure was only *3 times* higher in the 1970s than in the 1950s.)

In 1977, 60% of all children found guilty or cautioned were in trouble for theft or for handling stolen goods. A further 20% were in trouble for burglary. Vandalism and crimes of violence were only a small part of the total reported crime by young people – but these increased over the 1970s. More and more children were sent to detention centres and borstals during the decade.

The Children and Young Persons Act 1969 suggested that no one under age 14 should be charged with an offence, except in the case of murder. By the late 1970s the rule remained "no one under age 10". The Act suggested that the minimum age for a borstal sentence should be 17. By the late 1970s, the age for this was still 15. Other recommendations by the Act were that court for young people should be avoided. When possible, young offenders should be treated in their home setting instead of being locked up.

In Scotland, a Social Work (Scotland) Act was passed in 1968. This provided measures

4 Handforth Youth Club in Cheshire had a class for girls on how to resist assault. The rising number of attacks in the country prompted such courses. Girls learned self-defence from a local ex-commando (1979).

other than criminal proceedings for offenders under age 16. The Act came into force in 1971.

Young people helped put vandalism right as well. Heather McNeil (b. 1965), living near Glasgow: "There were underpasses outside the school with writing all over the walls. Older pupils who had taken art went and painted the walls over with nice colours and designs."

Gangs of youths made the headlines. In 1970 and '71 skinheads and Hell's Angels clashed with police at seaside resorts. One newspaper reported: "Police seize skinheads' braces." Shoelaces were taken as well, to keep things less active.

Hammersmith Teenage Project

The Hammersmith Teenage Project in London began in 1975, to work with those aged 12-16 who were either in trouble with the law, or at risk. Teenagers were assigned to project workers with the same sort of background as themselves. The project offered many activities. As one worker said, "A lot of the trouble that kids get into has to do with lack of leisure facilities. They need something to do and somewhere to go." Workers on the project also helped with homework, and counselled the teenagers and their parents.

Help for victims

There was also growing concern for *victims* of crime in the 1970s. The Criminal Justice Act 1972 allowed courts to award compensation, to be paid by offenders. Schemes for victims grew in a number of cities. These give emotional as well as financial help.

9

Did people change?

A MORI opinion poll in 1980 asked how life had changed over the Seventies. Depressingly, 86% of those asked thought that people were more aggressive.

76% thought that people were more selfish.
80% thought that people were less polite.
72% thought that people were less honest.
70% thought that people were less moral.
56% thought that people were less kind.
67% thought that people were less tolerant.

On a more cheerful note, 67% thought that people were more knowledgeable. 82% thought that people had become more open-minded.

From the mid-1970s young people were brought down-to-earth by hard realities, such as growing unemployment. The bright optimism of the 1960s seemed to fade. The headmaster of Winchester school wrote in *The Times* (1978) regretting that pupils had moved away from the idealism of the late Sixties.

Andy Alexander (b. 1960) thinks young people had less respect for their elders: "Young people were less willing to listen to their parents. They were less willing to be told."

5 and 6   A highlight of the Seventies was the Queen's Silver Jubilee in 1977, marking 25 years of her reign. During that year the Queen travelled around Britain meeting people. 7 June was Jubilee Day. Crowds watched as the Gold Coach took the Queen and Prince Philip to St Paul's Cathedral and then to the Guildhall. Children were treated to Jubilee parties, with long tables in the road and decorations. Sonya Wilson (b. 1968), living in South London: "At our council flats we had string with flags on it from one balcony to another. We had balloons stuck up as well. People brought out long tables and put out tons of food. Everyone came down and just enjoyed themselves. Someone blared out music and it lasted till night." Anood Shah (b. 1964), living in Harrow: "There was a community feeling. It created a family atmosphere on the whole street."

The Queen's Silver Jubilee Appeal was launched in 1977. Funds were raised to support projects with young people helping others.

2 Britain Divided

The Common Market

Many conflicts divided Britain in the 1970s. One big national issue was whether or not the UK should be in the European Economic Community (EEC) – the Common Market. In 1971 Prime Minister Edward Heath and the Conservatives were generally in favour of going *in* (as were the Liberals). The Labour Party was generally in favour of Britain staying *out*. The topic continued to be debated in Parliament. Entry was finally fixed for 1 January 1973.

Jane Elton (b. 1964) remembers projects at her primary school near Southampton on whether or not Britain should join. She also learned about other member countries.

Even after Britain had joined the Common Market, the debate did not stop. A referendum in 1975 posed the question: "Should the UK

7 Britain's anti-Common Market demonstrators made their feelings known to the President of France as he visited Prime Minister Heath for talks (1972).

11

stay in the EEC – Yes or No?" The result showed over 67% of people in favour of staying in, while over 32% wanted Britain out.

In 1979, Britain first elected Euro-MPs, to attend the European Parliament.

Northern Ireland

Another big conflict growing during the Seventies was over Northern Ireland. British troops had been sent to Ulster in 1969, to "keep the peace".

In 1970, television news showed children in Northern Ireland hurling dustbin lids and paving stones at soldiers and police. 1971 was an even worse year. Those dying in the violence included a 17-month-old baby. A British soldier (the first of many) was also killed.

A photo in 1971 newspapers showed a 19-year-old girl tied to a lamppost in Londonderry. Her head was shaved and her body tarred and feathered. This had been punishment for her going out with a British soldier, whom she later married. In 1974 two young girls were found, tied to railings, with their heads shaved. Round their necks were placards saying "self-confessed touts" (Ulster slang for informers).

There were bomb attacks on the UK mainland. Security was increased. Bag searches as people entered public buildings became routine. As violence continued, more troops were sent in. A plebiscite in March 1973 showed that the majority of people in Ulster wanted to remain part of the UK. It was minority Catholics who wanted Northern Ireland to be re-united with Ireland.

Two Irish women working to end the violence were awarded the Nobel Peace Prize in 1976. By the end of the decade, the issue of Northern Ireland was still unresolved. People on both sides felt *theirs* to be the just cause.

8   Northern Ireland, 1975. Stones and petrol bombs were hurled by Catholics and Protestants during a battle across the "Peace Line" in Belfast. Children took part in the battles and were sometimes injured or killed.

3 Energy, Transport and the Environment

Energy

"Energy" suddenly became a topic of worry in the 1970s. Many children heard the initials OPEC (Organization of Petroleum Exporting Countries) for the first time. OPEC put up the price of oil dramatically. The days of cheap fuel were over. Petroleum became much dearer over the decade and "energy-saving" was encouraged. Children noticed parents more serious about double-glazing windows, lagging lofts and saving heat generally. The Department of Energy launched its "SAVE-IT" campaign in 1975.

Britain itself became an oil-producing country in the 1970s. In June 1976 the first commercial North Sea oil came ashore. By

9 Britain's first solar-heated house (1975) in Milton Keynes, Buckinghamshire. The roof-top solar panels trap the sun's rays, absorbing heat. This heat is transferred in water to storage tanks – and then to the central heating and hot water systems. As the cost of oil soared in the 1970s, alternative energy sources were being considered much more seriously.

June 1978 oil production was topping a million barrels a day for the first time, meeting 60% of the country's needs.

Road travel

Motorways continued to expand. About twice the length of motorways were in use at the end of the 1970s as at the start. More and more children lived in families with the use of their own car. These increased from 51% of all families in 1971 to 58% by 1979.

Motorbikes were popular with teenagers. Andy Alexander (b. 1960): "If you could talk your Dad into putting his name on an HP agreement, you could have something like a small Honda 50."

Rail and air travel

There was a slight decline in the length of railway lines in Britain over the decade. However, trains did become much more modern and faster. British Rail launched its "Inter-City 125" fast passenger services in 1976.

Air travel took off in several new ways. Passenger services on *Concorde*, the first supersonic airliner, began in 1976. Laker's *Skytrain*, launched in 1977, offered cheaper fares across the Atlantic. This gave more young people the chance to fly to North America.

The environment

Environmental problems, both local and worldwide, were a focus of concern. Recycling, to save the earth's resources, was being encouraged. In 1971 the pressure group Friends of the Earth began a campaign against the waste of non-returnable bottles.

An enormous pile of empties was deposited on the steps of one drinks manufacturer. Many young people joined in such demonstrations and campaigns.

Scott Thomas (b. 1968), living in South Wales, remembers bottle banks starting. His parents were landlords of a pub. "There were a lot of empty bottles we used to take down there."

The Schools Eco-Action Group began in 1972 at a school in Berkshire. Pupils staged an exhibition, a litter pick-up and a campaign on packaging. The movement spread to include other schools acting on ecology issues.

National Trust Acorn Camps started in 1969. These were popular in the 1970s for young people wanting to help with conservation. The camps provided a working holiday, on which people helped to clear fallen timber and otherwise improve the countryside.

European Architectural Heritage Year in 1975 focused attention on Britain's old buildings and the need to conserve these.

In 1979 the Greenpeace conservation group carried a model whale across London's Tower Bridge as part of its "Save the Whale" campaign.

10 (1972) Young people were enrolled by the Department of the Environment as "Litter Defence Volunteers". The workers wore orange T-shirts and helped clean up after carnivals and pageants. This was all part of the drive in the 1970s to improve the environment.

4 Work, Unemployment and Strikes

Employment of Children Act 1973

In past years, young people in Britain often worked long hours in mills and mines. A series of laws began in the nineteenth century to give some protection. The Employment of Children Act 1973 said that no child under school-leaving age could be employed

*under 13 years of age

*before the close of school hours on any day on which he or she is required to attend school

*before 7 am or after 7 pm on any day

*for more than two hours on any day on which he or she is required to attend school

*for more than two hours on any Sunday

*to lift, carry or move anything so heavy as to be likely to cause injury to him or her.

Exceptions were made for some work, for example, where younger children might help their parents with light farm work. Since 1973 school-children are not allowed to do such jobs as working on machinery, in betting shops, selling petrol. Someone aged 13-16 wanting to work has to apply to the local education authority.

Jobs for children

The most popular part-time jobs for school-children in the 1970s were working in shops, cafes, or hairdressers' or doing newspaper- or milk-rounds. In 1977 one 14-year-old girl worked in a Sussex cafe, washing-up and waitressing for 50p an hour. A 13-year-old boy in London did a couple of newspaper rounds and earned £12 a week. A 15-year-old boy was paid 60p an hour in a butcher's shop for taking meat out of the cold store for display.

These rates of pay were not too bad for the time. However, many children were working in bad conditions for much lower pay. Also in 1977, 15-year-old boys worked at a handbag factory in East London every evening, earning just 20p-30p an hour. One Derby girl aged 15 worked all evening in a snack bar for a total of 60p, with no tips. Sometimes employers were brought to court.

The law was being broken by school-children anxious to earn some money and by employers looking for cheap labour. As the boys working at the handbag factory put it, "You can't go asking for money at home all the time."

Spending money and savings

In 1970 British children's pocket money totalled a staggering £125 million. Those aged 10-15 spent nearly a tenth of their money on clothes and going to the cinema. Older girls spent £3 million a year on cosmetics. Boys were spending the same amount to go to watch football. Records, stamps and model kits were other temptations.

A 1975/76 survey on pocket money, including money received for jobs, showed about a third of 13-16-year-olds receiving over £2 a week. Another third received between £1 and £2. IPC magazines surveyed girls aged 12-18 in 1977. The average pocket money for a girl of 12 was £1 a week. Nearly two-thirds of 16-18-year-old girls had a savings account of some kind.

Not everyone felt like saving. Andy Alexander (b. 1960) had his first real job at 16, in a fishmonger's, earning £26 a week. "You used to just spend your wages as it went, having as much fun as possible. Came Thursday you had no money left."

Teenagers in the decade were big spenders. Manufacturers realized how important this growing market was. In 1976 teenage spendable income was over £1,072 million. Over £47 million was spent on cosmetics and toiletries, £35 million on sweets, £22 million on denim jeans and skirts, and £13 million on crisps and peanuts.

Industrial action

Strikes were not invented in the 1970s, but the decade seemed to have more than its share. All this industrial action was noticed by and even copied by young people.

11 Members of the "Devil's Henchmen" gang helped deliver YMCA mail in London during the first-ever strike by postal workers in 1971. Many post boxes were sealed-up during the six weeks of action.

(Andy Alexander (b. 1960), living in London, remembers another Hell's Angels gang called "the Road Rats": "We used to stay clear of them. They were scarey.")

12 A young secretary manages to keep typing in a London office, 1972. Homes, factories, shops and offices were plunged into periodic darknesses because of the miners' strike.

In 1972 a newspaper reported on three children aged 11, 12 and 6 who staged a walk-out from their home "because they reckoned they were overworked and underpaid". They left a note saying: "Dear Mum, we love you very much but we don't get enough pocket money and we have to do little jobs we don't like, like cleaning and washing-up." After 48 hours living rough, the children returned home. They were "delighted to declare an unconditional return to work."

A "state of emergency" was declared by the government twice during 1970. In July this was because of action by the dockers, and in December because of action by power workers. Throughout the year teachers, dockers, miners, car workers and power workers were either on strike or working to rule. By October 1970, more working days had been lost through strikes than in any year since 1926 (the time of the General Strike).

1972 was another difficult year. The number

of working days lost from strikes was nearly twice the number lost in 1971. By the end of January 1972 the miners were on official strike. A state of emergency was declared with vital supplies and services disrupted. Power cuts were introduced and over 1½ million workers in other industries were laid off. The gloomy newspaper headlines of 11 February read: "All Britain on Half-time – Millions to be Laid Off", "3-Day Working Week By Law!", "Big Shutdown on the Way", "Big Switch Off Blacks Out Millions", "Blacked Out and Laid Off" . . .

Sonya Wilson (b. 1968), living in London, recalls how scarey it was for a small child. "Sometimes the lights in the whole block of flats would just go off. My mother had to light candles." Jane Elton (b. 1965), living near Southampton: "My father took a car battery and attached a lamp to it. We used to go to bed a bit earlier. There wasn't anything to do. You couldn't watch television."

The miners were working again by the end of February 1972. However, five months later, another state of emergency was declared. This time it was because of a national dock strike. Another big strike of the year was in the building industry.

As a result of industrial action, 1974 began with the country's working week reduced to three days. Drivers were forbidden to exceed 50 mph, as a way of saving petrol. There were other restrictions on the use of fuel for heating, lighting and advertising.

1979 had the worst winter weather for 16 years. This combined with what seemed like an endless series of strikes and go-slows.

Unemployment
Alongside industrial unrest, the jobless toll was rising. In 1971 the rate of unemployment was growing more quickly than in any year since 1946. By the end of January 1972, the number of people without jobs reached over a million for the first time since 1947. The number of unemployed rose from 0.7 million in 1971 to 1.3 million by 1979.

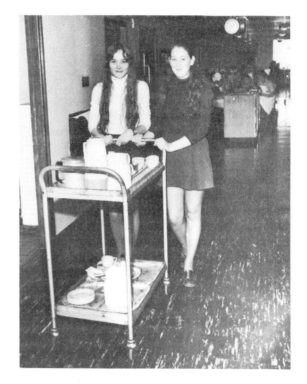

13   Thousands of hospital workers staged a one-day strike for more pay in 1972. Some London schoolchildren, like those in the photo, were called in to help carry out essential duties in the hospitals affected.

14   School leavers studied the job board at a new "Job Shop" at Thames Polytechnic, Woolwich, in 1979. Some young people were facing extra problems. Ethnic minority workers were more likely to have difficulty in finding jobs. Between 1975 and 1978, unemployment amongst ethnic minorities under age 25 rose by 186%, compared with an overall increase for the age group of 97%.

Growing up in the 1970s meant that you were increasingly likely to use and see goods that were made outside the UK. As you came out of school, you had less chance of getting a job in manufacturing industry. Its decline, which had started years before, was continuing. During the decade more and more manufactured goods were being imported from other countries. Of all manufactured goods that children saw around them in Britain, about 17% were from other countries in 1970. This was up to nearly 26% by 1979.

Youth Opportunities Programme

From 1972 to 1978, unemployment amongst young people rose three times as fast as total unemployment. A report called *Young People and Work* was published in 1976 by the government's Manpower Services Commission. A new "Youth Opportunities Programme" was announced in early 1978 to try to relieve the growing problem. In that year YOP was to provide over 200,000 16-, 17- and 18-year-olds with the chance of six months' training and work experience. YOP was available to any young person under age 19 who had been unemployed for six weeks or more. All were paid a standard allowance of £19.50 a week by the government, from 1 April 1978.

Advertisements urged businesses to join the scheme: "There are now more young people out of work than at any time since the war. In some areas it is one in three." A focus for YOP schemes were the six key areas where 45% of Britain's young unemployed were living – Strathclyde, Tyne and Wear, Merseyside, Manchester, West Midlands and London.

Some teenagers were taken on as permanent staff after their work experience with a firm. This happened to Cheryl, who was at a motorworks in Shrewsbury. She described the depressing picture facing so many young people in 1978: "After I left school I went on the dole and carried on looking for work. The more I looked, the more depressed I got. I wanted to be a receptionist or secretary but they wanted people with experience . . ."

YOP served some useful purposes, but there were criticisms of it as well. Some employers made use of YOP as a source of free labour, instead of hiring workers at normal rates. In some cases young people were not receiving any really useful training. Another problem was that after six months on a YOP placement, a young person might well just find him or

15   Ten unemployed young people from Cardiff worked for the Welsh Industrial and Maritime Museum, reconstructing the world's first steam locomotive. This was part of the new MSC's Youth Opportunities Programme. (1978).

herself on the dole again. A new Youth Training Scheme replaced YOP in 1982, trying to improve on what was offered to young people in the late 1970s.

Community Action Teams

A variety of schemes developed in the late '70s to employ young people. Community Action teams were popular in Sunderland. Each team had four boys and four girls and a supervisor. Old people wanting house decorating or minor repairs done could request help. The old people paid for materials and young people were paid by the government to do the work.

One girl, Andrea, hoped to use the skills she was learning to become a self-employed decorator. She said in 1978: "You can see the old people really happy when they've had their house done. They send letters congratulating us."

Community Industry

Another government-supported scheme in Sunderland was run by "Community Industry". Besides organizing painting, decorating and landscaping projects, it also ran workshops for woodwork and needlework. Dolly, in the needlework workshop, explained in 1978: "We recycle old clothes for old people and little children . . . We also make toys for children, cushions, curtains, lots of other things . . ."

Toy Workshop

Also busy employing young people in 1978 was the Hackney Under-Fives' Toy Workshop in London. Teenagers helped build toys for young children – and helped design them as well.

"Just the Job"

Another project, "Just the Job", began in 1977 with sponsorship from the Manpower Services Commission. This tried to help the young rural unemployed in Devon and Cornwall. The idea was to combine television programmes, information kits and group counselling about how best to find a job. After a Westward

Television series attracted interest, adult counsellors ran weekly groups with YUPs (Young Unemployed Persons). Hundreds of teenagers found this helpful. Some found places on WEPs (Work Experience Programmes).

Voluntary work

Many teenagers opted for doing voluntary work. In some cases they were paid a small amount. CSV, Community Service Volunteers, had a variety of projects. On the main programme, volunteers worked away from home and received pocket money, board, lodging and travelling expenses. On the "Springboard" scheme, teenagers worked locally and received a training allowance.

16   Young people in Surrey collected old clothes for charity on a Saturday morning, 1971.

Young people were doing such jobs as helping in old people's homes, working with mentally handicapped children and supervising at adventure playgrounds. Often the voluntary work gave experience and ideas for a permanent job.

Teenagers volunteered to help with the environment as well. The British Trust for Conservation Volunteers organized young people on projects, in cities as well as the countryside. Sometimes they were on job creation schemes funded by the government and so were receiving some pay. Andy, one teenager on a scheme in 1978, explained the appeal: "There's a sort of community spirit as you get everybody working alongside clearing a stream and it's pelting down with rain. You're still having a good laugh because there's that many there. . . . There is something at the end. They can see what they've done."

Some young people worked for free, as volunteers for charity. Sue was an 18-year-old volunteer at an Oxfam shop in Leamington Spa. She said in 1978: "I'd heard a lot about the problems facing young people. It wasn't until I started writing for jobs and getting to the interview stage and then finding out there were perhaps a hundred other applicants that I realized. . ."

5 Family and Home Life

Family life changed dramatically over the 1970s. There were fewer large families, more families with just a single parent, and many more mothers in paid employment. This combined with there being simply fewer children. The total number of children in Britain began to fall in 1971. It was not until the late 1970s that the number of births began to increase again.

Divorce
The number of divorces in Britain nearly doubled over the 1970s – from over 79,000 in 1971 to over 148,000 in 1979. The first divorce-by-post in Britain was granted in 1973. This was part of the whole process being made easier. The divorce rate reached 12 per 1,000 married couples in 1980. This was twice the 1971 rate and three times the rate of 1968.

Increased divorce and second marriages meant that many more children were living in single-parent homes or with step parents, and sometimes half-brothers and sisters. Families and family life became much more complicated for many people.

One-parent families
Between 1971 and 1979, the number of one-parent families in the UK increased from 570,000 to 900,000. By the end of the decade, 10% of children were living in single-parent families for at least some time. The rise was due mainly to the increase in divorce and separations, but also to the fact that more unmarried mothers were bringing up their own child. (The number of children adopted fell by half over the 1970s.)

The government's 1974 Finer Report on one-parent families suggested that they needed more help financially. The report also stressed the need for more day-care places for children, to help working lone parents.

"Gingerbread" was formed in 1970 to help single parents. In 1975 the organization held a

17 In 1973 three-year-old Caroline was finally back with her mother after a 27-month "tug-of-love" battle. As divorce increased, more children found themselves part of these struggles. Sometimes children were kidnapped out of the country by one parent.

big demonstration in London, with parents and children marching to Parliament. 40% of Britain's one-parent families were living at poverty level on supplementary benefit. 15% of one-parent families were living *below* the official poverty line. One-parent families were three times as likely to become homeless as two-parent families. A quarter of the children aged 11 living in one-parent families were having to share a bed. Over 300 self-help local Gingerbread groups were running by the late 1970s. One-parent families were helping each other and raising funds to pay for parties and outings.

Women working

An important social change over the decade was the increase in wives working outside the home. The number of children with working mothers went up by a third between 1971 and 1976. Many of the women worked part-time. Heather McNeil (b. 1966) was living near Glasgow: "My mum started working when I was nine. It was part-time, till we got older."

In 1976, nearly half of children under age 16 had mothers in paid employment. A quarter of these mothers worked full-time. There was growing concern about the shortage of child-care provision. The number of "latchkey" children was growing. By 1979, about 300,000 children were left alone either after school and/or in school holidays.

Child care

Childminders were the form of care most commonly used by working mothers in the 1970s. In 1977 childminders in Britain were registered to receive nearly 90,000 children either full- or part-time. Many childminders were not registered, and this meant that they might be uninsured and be taking more children than could be cared for properly. An estimated 100,000-300,000 children were with *un*registered minders.

Women's Lib

The Women's Movement burst upon Britain in

18   In 1971 the first Women's Liberation march in Britain went from Hyde Park to Trafalgar Square, with over 1,000 people. This included carried babies and children in push-chairs. A petition handed in to the Prime Minister called for free 24-hour child care centres, equal educational and job opportunities, equal pay, free contraception and abortion on demand.

the 1970s. Throughout the decade children were aware of women campaigning for more equal rights and opportunities.

There were constant "firsts" for women. In 1973 the London Stock Exchange accepted women members for the first time. In 1975 there was Britain's first woman jockey and the first woman jet airline captain. In 1976 Britain's first woman fireman and the first woman to serve as a British Ambassador were added. Women were entering more and more occupations that had been mainly or even almost exclusively male. The Sex Discrimination Act of 1975 made it illegal to discriminate against women in many areas of life. An Equal Opportunities Commission was set up to enforce the Act. 1975 was International Women's Year, starting a UN Decade to improve opportunities for women worldwide.

What is "manhood"?

Changing roles for men and women were a great concern of the decade. In 1972 a Sunday newspaper colour supplement devoted a whole issue to "What's Next for Manhood?" This included asking some 14-year-olds what they thought "manhood" meant. One said: "It's no longer necessary to try to be superhuman in

19 (1975) Many children became used to seeing fathers helping with tasks traditionally regarded as "women's work". The Women's Movement encouraged more sharing of house jobs.

(Stripped pine dressers and tables were part of a Seventies' fashion for "country" furniture and more "natural" living.)

that old-fashioned way. Now it is possible to be an individual, yourself. I don't think manhood, in the old sense, will ever come back."

Co-habitation

Couples living together outside of marriage is hardly a new idea. But of women who married in Britain in the late 1960s, only 1% had lived with their husbands first. By the early 1970s this figure had jumped to 9%. By 1979, the General Household Survey found that the proportion of couples living together before their wedding had soared to 20%. Co-habitation became much more socially acceptable over the 1970s, at least to the young.

As more couples "lived together" in the 1970s, the rate of marriage fell. More babies were registered as born to an unmarried couple. Most people who did co-habit did eventually marry – but later, on average, than in the 1960s. A teenage girl at the *end* of the 1970s was only half as likely to be married as a teenage girl at the *start* of the decade.

Sex and contraceptives

Contraceptives for birth control became much more easily available. This was a factor in the lowering of the birth rate. Oral contraceptives ("the pill") had been sold in Britain since 1961 – but it was 1972 before birth control became available free, paid for by the rates. Contraceptives became available to all over age 16, married or not.

Children growing up in the 1970s were exposed to much franker attitudes to sex generally. The first topless newspaper pin-up appeared in 1970. Surveys suggested that more young people were having sexual relations at an early age. A mid-1960s survey had shown 6% of 15-year-old boys and 2½% of 15-year-old girls claiming to be sexually experienced. By a mid-1970s survey, 25% of boys and 12% of girls aged 15 made this claim. "Friends" continued to be the main source of information, but in the 1970s more young people mentioned parents and teachers as well. There were campaigns for more and better sex education in schools.

In 1970 the Health Education Council launched a campaign to prevent unwanted children. The eye-catching poster showed a full-stomached *man*. The message to males was that they would be more careful about contraception if *they* could become pregnant.

Children's Act 1975

Changes made by the 1975 Children's Act have given more security to children in foster families. The Act has also made it easier for children "in care" to find adoptive families. It helped transform the whole pattern of adoption.

In the mid-1970s, adoption was still mainly a service providing babies, often illegitimate, to childless couples. By the 1980s, it became much more a service finding families for children in need, often with social or physical handicaps.

The people who adopted children changed over the 1970s as well. More of them than before already had children of their own. Also, more children were being placed with single people. Agencies began more often to place black children with black families. Greater use was made of television, radio and newspapers to recruit adoptive families generally. The first television programme showing children needing homes was shown in 1974.

A controversial part of the 1975 Act was that it allowed adopted people the right, for the first time, to find out who their real parents were.

The 1975 Act also changed parental rights. Until then, parents and children were regarded as one unit. This did not work for some children, such as those being abused. The Act said that children's interests could need to be separate.

20 London schoolchildren visited an old people's home to give gifts as part of their Harvest Festival in 1971. Fewer old people than before were living with their children and grandchildren. The proportion of old people continued to increase, from just over 16% of the population at the start of the Seventies to just over 17% by the end of the decade.

21 (1972) New "whistle seats" were filled with urethane foam rubber. Furniture styles became more casual to match more casual homes and styles of living.

Heating and appliances

Homes changed as well as the families in them. Central heating increased from being in only 32% of homes in 1971 to being in 55% by 1979. The telephone became more common, too. Only 38% of homes had a telephone in 1971, compared to 67% by 1979. Heather McNeil (b. 1966), near Glasgow: "We got our first telephone when I was about 12. I phoned all my friends, gave everyone my number. It was very exciting."

Homes were using more and more electrical appliances and gadgets. Ownership of refrigerators increased from 72% of households in 1971 to 95% in 1979. Washing machines were in only 64% of homes in 1971, but in 77% of homes by 1979.

Homelessness

Homelessness was a growing problem over the 1970s, and was highlighted by pressure groups like SHELTER. In 1970 the number of homeless households in England and Wales asking for help from local authorities was 26,000. This had doubled by 1977. There were over 1,300 children separated from their parents in 1976 because the family was homeless.

Besides children living in homeless families, there was an increasing number of young people homeless on their own. The Campaign for the Homeless and Rootless (CHAR) in 1975 drew attention to the growing number of children flocking in to London from the provinces. In 1976 a report estimated that 8,000 homeless young people were sleeping out rough in London over Christmas.

High-rise flats

Criticism of high-rise flats grew, especially those used for families with young children.

The National Society for the Prevention of Cruelty to Children (NSPCC) warned in 1970 that small children brought up in such flats could become retarded. They were much more restricted than other children and play facilities were poor. By 1979 there were 300,000 children living in flats above second-floor level.

Drought of '76

A crisis occurred in summer 1976, with weather the sunniest for 500 years. Shortage of rain over the spring and summer prompted a "Drought Act" which came into force by August. Parts of the country were able to draw water for only a few hours a day. Water to industry was restricted.

Many home-owners had to draw water from standpipes in the street. Adults and children arrived to fill their buckets and tubs. Scott Thomas (b. 1968), living in South Wales: "For the worst couple of weeks it was getting out the old pots, anything that could hold water. You could only wash clothes once a week. You used to feel a bit guilty having a glass of squash which you filled up with water."

There were restrictions on using sprinklers and washing cars. Debbie Tyldesley (b. 1966) was living in Bournemouth at the time: "There were helicopters going over. You were fined for watering your garden when you shouldn't."

Water was used, and re-used. Several people would use the same bath water, and then this would be used to water plants. Scott Thomas (b. 1968): "Once I pulled the plug out of the bath without asking if anyone else wanted the water. No one else in the house could bathe for the rest of the day. I was in a bit of trouble for that."

The Minister for Sport was temporarily appointed "Minister for Drought". Rains finally came and full supplies were restored near the end of September.

22 (1971) Children on a North London council estate cheered a friend who was to appear in a television film. Over the 1970s, slightly more homes (such as the flats shown) were being rented from local authorities (31%-32% of all housing). Fewer children were living in homes rented from private landlords. More children lived in homes that their families were buying rather than renting. Only 50% of UK homes were owner-occupied in 1971 – but this was up to 55% by 1979.

6 Health, Welfare and Food

Overall, the 1970s was a decade of increasing good health for Britain. People were living longer, on average, at the end of the 1970s than at the start. Life expectancy rose, for men, from over 68 years in 1971 to over 70 years by 1979. For women, the increase was from 75 years to over 76 years.

At the same time, a smaller percentage of babies were dying, per 1,000 live births. The infant mortality rate fell sharply, from 17.9 in 1971 to 12.9 by 1979. The chances for babies from poorer homes were less good than those from richer homes.

Test-tube babies

New advances such as "test-tube babies" became a reality. This helped couples unable to conceive in the usual way. The world's very first test-tube baby was born in Oldham, England, on 25 July 1978. Louise Brown was produced by taking a ripe egg from the wife's ovary and putting it in a culture dish along with sperm from the husband. The embryo was allowed to develop for two and a half days and then placed inside the mother's uterus to continue growing. Many more test-tube babies have followed since.

Health services

Health visitors were seeing about 10% fewer young children in their homes than in the 1960s. By the end of the 1970s, about half of those under age five were being taken to child health clinics each year. Children from poorer

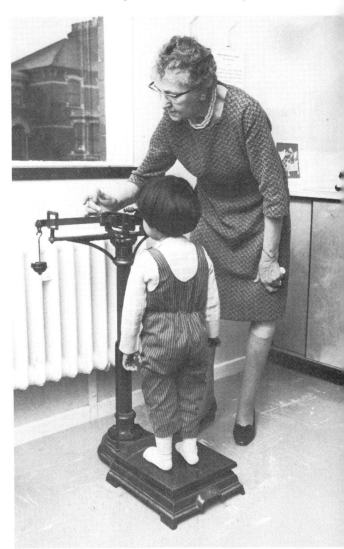

23 In 1971 London's borough of Lewisham opened its first comprehensive Health Centre. Family doctors and dentists were based there. Services included vaccination, child health care and family planning. Ante- and post-natal clinics were added, as were a child guidance unit and a creche for children while mothers were being attended. There were few of these Health Centres in Britain until the mid-1960s. From then, the idea spread. By 1972 there were over 500 centres in the UK.

families were much less likely to attend. 90% of children under age five were seeing their GP every year. This was true for about 60% of children aged 5-14 as well.

Vaccination against whooping cough became controversial. Some children suffered brain damage as a result of immunization. Parents were urged to continue having their children vaccinated, as the benefits far outweighed the risks.

Accidents

Diseases such as cancers, heart disease and respiratory disease were an increasing problem over the 1970s. By contrast, the number of road accidents did decline. However, *for children over age one*, accidents of all kinds were the main cause of death. Accidents were the cause of nearly 30% of deaths in the 1-4 age-group. Nearly 20% of 5-14-year-olds who died did so as a result of road accidents. A 1977 report showed that half of all accidents occurring in the home were to children.

The Health and Safety Executive launched a major campaign in 1977 to stop children trespassing on building sites. A film called *Building Sites Bite* was shown widely. In the film, a 13-year-old boy pretended to lie crushed beneath a fallen pile of bricks. This was a common accident on construction sites.

Children from poorer homes were much more likely than others to suffer from accidents. The rate of deaths due to falls, fires and drownings was over ten times higher for boys in the lowest economic group than for boys from the richest families.

Bonfire Night firework injuries to children continued to cause concern. "Child maiming season is here again," warned a newspaper headline in October 1972.

24 **The British Safety Council was concerned with reducing injuries. In 1979 over 350 children from all over Britain met on London's South Bank to paint the longest safety poster in the world. Teams of three from different schools each completed a section showing an aspect of safety from 1000 BC to the present day. The winning team with the best painting received a cheque for £500 and a trophy.**

Child abuse

The problem of *deliberate* injury to children continued in the 1970s. One estimate in the late 1970s was that 7,000-8,000 children under age 16 were being "non-accidentally" injured each year. This included about 100 deaths and over 1,500 serious injuries.

In 1977, over 100 people in England and Wales were found guilty in a magistrates' court of cruelty to a child, not including murder or serious assaults. In addition, the juvenile courts had over 4,600 proceedings to take children into care on the grounds that they were being ill-treated or neglected. In 1976 the NSPCC published a report on parental violence and called for a register of children at risk. In 1977 they called for special "battered child" units to be set up in major towns and cities.

Family violence

Children did not need to be hit themselves to be affected by violence in the home. One woman beaten by her husband explained in 1977: "My boy had to go for psychiatric treatment every week. The girl always looked after me. She'd wash the wounds and all. But the boy, if there was a big fight in the evening, the following day it would all come out of him at school."

Family violence caused growing concern. Chiswick Women's Aid in London was started in 1972 as a house refuge for battered wives (This became Chiswick Family Refuge in 1978.) A National Women's Aid Federation was formed by thirty Women's Aid groups in 1975. By 1977 there were over one hundred groups all over the UK. Seventy-four of these had at least one refuge to take in battered wives and their children.

Children in care

Fewer than 1% of children in England and Wales were in the "care" of local authorities in the 1970s. The Children Act 1948 gave courts the power to put into care children with no parents or those whose parents are unable to look after them. The Children and Young Persons Act 1979 widened this to add children who offend criminally or who are in need of care and control. By the end of the 1970s, about 100,000 children were in care at any one time, some for a short period only.

Stress and suicide

Growing stress amongst young people, sometimes leading to suicide, was yet another worry in the decade. In 1979 one girl killed herself because of anxiety over a cooking exam. In 1974 one boy who could not face the extra compulsory year at school, when the leaving age was raised, hanged himself. Growing divorce rates and unemployment added to the pressures felt by some young people. One 16-year-old boy committed suicide in 1976 because he could not find a job. The boy's father said at the time: "This was a case of a boy feeling as if he was on the scrapheap – a boy whose self-respect and pride had been wrecked, who felt totally rejected."

Drugs and "sniffing"

Over the years 1971-77 the number of notified drug addicts under the age of 20 actually went down. This may have meant that fewer young people were using hard drugs, or that more drugs were being bought illegally. John Alexander (b. 1958) was at a fee-paying school near Oxford. "It was mild drugs mainly cannabis, at the school. They were at it all the time."

Alternatives to drug-taking seemed to increase over the Seventies. There were over 50 deaths of children and teenagers from "glue-sniffing", or solvent abuse, in England and Scotland between 1970 and 1977. In addition, other young people suffered damage to their health as a result of "glue-sniffing". Over the decade, a younger and younger age group became involved. By 1977 there were even cases of five- and six-year-olds in Scotland inhaling glue and aerosol sprays. Heather McNeil (b. 1965), living near Glasgow: "There were quite a few people at my school who were glue-sniffing. They had scars round their mouth and looked funny. They were sort of drunk, as if they didn't know what they were doing."

Drinking

Increased alcoholic drinking by young

26 **Skinheads waited for a pub to open, 1970. Teenage drinking, especially under-age drinking, was of growing concern over the decade.**

Skinheads were mainly a late 1960s', early 1970s' fashion – but continued over the decade as well. The uniform included Dr Martin boots, somewhat short trousers, braces and closely cropped hair. Andy Alexander (b. 1960): "After the film *Clockwork Orange* in 1971, skinheads were going about with steel toe-capped boots. It was all 'I'm wearing steel toe caps and I'm dangerous'."

teenagers over the 1970s was another issue. Newspapers talked of "the cocktail kids" and "the teeny-drunks". Andy Alexander (b. 1960): "I was 11 when I first got drunk. We used to drink a bottle of cider each. We had this little camp on an empty site. . ."

The number of people under age 18 found guilty of public drunkenness was 5,400 in 1977 – over twice the 1968 number.

A 1976 survey on drinking found 90% of 13-16-year-olds claiming to drink alcohol on licensed premises and/or at home. 10-15% claimed to have been "very drunk" more than once in the previous year. In 1979 supermarkets announced a new scheme to try to stop minors buying alcoholic drinks.

John Alexander (b. 1958), at school near Oxford: "If we did have a few pounds in our pocket, it was down to the pub. We were all under age."

Smoking

The danger to health from smoking became widely publicized over the 1970s. There was

27 Gormit Singh and Anna-Marie Riley modelled a new hearing aid harness to help the over 12,000 deaf children then in Britain (1977).

growing concern about the number of people with the habit. Doctors called for more attempts to prevent children ever starting to smoke. In 1977, ASH, the pressure group against smoking, began campaigning against the illegal but widespread sale of cigarettes to those under age 16.

The handicapped

In the mid-1970s, about 5% of children aged up to four years and about 10% of those aged 5-16 were moderately or severely handicapped. This included physical, motor, visual, hearing and communications or learning disorders needing special health care. Over the 1970s, more and more families of the mentally handicapped (about 1 in every 250 children under age 16) kept them at home instead of putting them in long-term institutions.

A settlement was reached in 1973 on the thalidomide baby cases. A number of women who had taken the thalidomide drug during pregnancy had produced deformed children. After a bitter court struggle, the drug manufacturers gave some compensation.

Government benefits

Family allowances started in the late 1940s as government payments to help families with more than one child. A new payment called Child Benefit began in 1979, replacing the family allowance. The new CB payments were made for *every* child in the country – even the first in a family, and rich children as well as poor.

In 1971, a new benefit called Family Income Supplement was started to help the poorest third to half of poor families with children.

The Child Poverty Action Group started in the mid-1960s. It drew attention in the 1970s to the increasing number of deprived children in Britain. In 1978 half a million children lived in families where income was below the official poverty level, even though one or both parents worked full-time. Another one million children lived in families depending on Supplementary Benefit because the head of

28 In 1972, poor children were treated to a day in Southend by London taxi drivers. The number of children living in families on or below the government's "poverty line" rose over the decade.

the family was sick, unemployed or elderly or a single parent.

Food trends

Food surveys during the decade revealed a number of trends. For example, children and adults were eating fewer cooked breakfasts, more snacks and fewer proper meals. Family meals tended to become less formal. For Gary Hollander-Woods (b. 1961), living in Lincolnshire, (and for many other young people), meals were often off a tray on your knees, in front of the "telly".

Many families were buying less fresh food. More convenience foods such as canned soups, were being eaten. Convenience foods need only final preparation by the shopper. By the late 1970s Britain was also well into the age of fast foods needing no preparation by the shopper at all.

The amount of frozen foods eaten in the UK rose dramatically over the Seventies. Only 26% of homes had a freezer in 1975 but this was 50% by 1980. Children were eating more frozen vegetables, frozen meat and fish products, and more frozen fruits and desserts over the decade.

Take-away meals

A newspaper article in 1972 was headed

"Take-away Meals Take Off". The number of take-away food shops – selling cooked meals from pizzas and hamburgers to kebabs, Chinese and Indian – was expanding rapidly. Children were becoming used to these, along with the traditional fish and chips.

"Kentucky Fried Chicken" was just one of the American-style fast food chains that became widespread over the 1970s. The chain was actually created in the USA as long ago as 1939, but it was 1965 before one "Kentucky Fried Chicken" shop opened in Britain. More appeared only slowly until 1971 when there were 85 branches. By the end of 1972 this number had nearly doubled, with 90 in London alone. Andy Alexander (b. 1960): "The greatest thing after a party or something was you'd all go round 'Kentucky'. Chicken and chips. Lovely."

Along with the increase in take-away food came more litter on the streets. This problem was raised in the House of Commons in 1975.

Fitness and diet

Over the 1970s awareness increased of the links between good diet and healthy living. In 1976 there were calls for a national nutrition campaign.

People were being urged to eat less saturated fat, less sugar and more fibre. High-fibre bran cereals became fashionable, as did jogging and exercise generally. Date-stamping of perishable foods began in the mid-1970s. Fuller labelling of food contents also became required.

Sweets, ice-cream and soft drinks

A "Food Facts" report by the Ministry of Agriculture in 1973 noted that children in Britain were eating more ice-cream and drinking more soft drinks than ever before. A survey of children's pocket money in 1970 found children spending about a fifth of their money on confectionery and ice-cream. Children aged 5-9 were spending over a third of their money on these. Consumption of sugar in such foods and drinks had gone up markedly

29 A new shopping centre at Reading in Berkshire (1972) was part of a growing trend. Such centres included supermarkets as well as other shops. More large discount stores also appeared, as did frozen food centres for bulk-buying. Gary Hollander-Woods (b. 1961), living in Lincolnshire, recalls eating more meat after his family bought a freezer. "You would buy a whole side of beef. . ."

30 A number of "baby snatchings" occurred in the early 1970s. Babies were stolen from prams left outside supermarkets. In 1974, one chain of stores offered papoose-style slings for use by mothers as they shopped.

since the 1950s. By the age of five, 70% of children already had some tooth decay – and 97% by the age of 15.

Anood Shah (b. 1964): "I used to get Jamboree bags with a few sweets and little plastic novelties inside."

Crisps were the most popular item bought in school tuck shops in 1971, followed by chocolate biscuits. Heather McNeil (b. 1965), who lived near Glasgow, remembers having a weakness for "mainly crisps" and "anything chocolate". A 1971 survey showed that children were spending more money on such snacks and eating tuck more often.

Soft drinks took on a new look in the 1970s. Aluminium cans were first used for these drinks in the UK by Tizer in 1975. In 1977 a drink called "Jubilade" was produced for the Queen's Silver Jubilee. This was a strawberry-flavoured sugar drink, tinned and fizzy.

Soya and school meals

In the mid-1970s, soya "meat" substitute products began to appear widely in supermarkets. The protein-rich soya bean is much cheaper to produce and healthier in some ways than meat. Soya can be made into "meat-like" mince and chunks. Many school-children were being given this "artificial" meat for lunch and did not seem to notice. "Derbyshire children to eat soya in school meals," read one 1975 headline.

School meals have been an on-going service since 1906. Their importance to the nutrition of many children was noted in a report by the Department of Education and Science in 1975: "There are still children whose only adequate meal of the day is the one they get at school."

Those claiming free school meals were over a million in 1978. Some other children who were poor enough to qualify were not claiming. The Child Poverty Action Group campaigned in the 1970s (and still in the 1980s) for free school meals for *all* children, to avoid the poor feeling embarrassed.

31 Wolverhampton, 1970. School meals were taken by more children in the 1970s, before the 1980 Education Act. This Act reduced the number of children entitled to free meals.

7 Education and Schools

Likes and dislikes

On the whole, 1970s surveys showed pupils fairly satisfied with their education. *Cricket and Company*, a children's magazine with competitions every month, in 1975 invited under-nines to write in, "I like school because. . ." and "I don't like school because. . .". Among the dislikes, nearly every Scottish child worried about punishment by "the belt". School dinners and teachers shouting were not terribly popular either. The likes were many, including nice teachers, PE, drawing and painting, making things and drama. For one eight-year-old, the highlight of school was "cleaning the blackboard if there is a lot of things on it".

Truancy

Some children who *didn't* like school simply did not turn up. This was most a problem in the larger cities, and some schools had an especially bad record. In 1972 one tabloid newspaper featured a "shock" report noting that every week in Britain over a million children were playing truant. One London 13-year-old, Paul, spent much time just wandering, trainspotting or going to museums. Paul: "What I can't stand is the boredom. It's like being locked in the cupboard under the stairs but not being frightened, just sort of walled in."

The final compulsory year at school seemed to be the worst for truancy. Age 15 was the most common age according to a survey by the Inner London Education Authority. Andy Alexander (b. 1960): "I hardly went to school the last year at all. I just worked in this cafe,

32 In 1972 over 350,000 people signed a petition for more nursery classes. This was taken to the House of Commons by mothers and young children. The National Campaign for Nursery Education was an active pressure group in the Seventies. Over the decade, a higher proportion of children and young people – from the youngest to the oldest – were in education. The percentage of children aged two to four in nursery schools more than doubled.

earning £2.50 a day. I used to love working rather than sitting at school."

Raised leaving age

At the start of the 1970s, about 60% of pupils left school at the earliest legal time – age 15. The idea of raising this to 16 stemmed from the 1944 Education Act and was supported by reports in the 1950s and '60s. The plan was to raise the age in 1970-71, but in 1968 this was delayed. It was not until 1972-73 that the school-leaving age became 16.

By 1979, 70% of 16-year-olds allowed to leave school were doing so – but a fifth of these went on to other kinds of full-time education. The percentage of 16-17-year-olds in full-time education increased from 28% in 1971 to 36% by 1979 at schools, and from 6% to 10% at further education colleges.

By the end of the decade, the proportion of 18-year-olds in full-time education was nearly three times what it had been in 1960. The percentage of 18-20-year-olds at university increased from just over 5% to just over 6% during the 1970s.

Open University

The Open University began teaching in 1971, in co-operation with the BBC. The OU was meant for the many adults in Britain who wanted to take degree courses, but who had not been able to go to university. Viewers could watch lectures on television and take a degree largely by post. OU graduates were first awarded degrees in 1973.

Children found that not only their parents, but sometimes also their grandparents were enrolled. One 81-year-old received her degree in 1977. She said that taking the course made a bond with her grandchildren who were doing "O" and "A" levels at the time. They encouraged her.

Exams

Young people in the 1970s continued to take the Certificate of Secondary Education (CSE) exams, usually at age 16. These exams started in 1965 in England and Wales, but not until 1973 in Northern Ireland. In England and

33 In 1970 girls were admitted to the King's School, Ely, Cambridgeshire, for the first time in the school's one-thousand-year history. There was a sharp decline in single-sex schools during the 1970s. In 1968 there were 1,071 girls' and 1,066 boys' schools. By 1981 this was down to 415 for girls only and 391 for boys only. In 1974 five men's colleges at Oxford University admitted women for the first time.

Wales there were also the General Certificate of Education (GCE) "O" level exams, also usually taken at age 16. Further GCEs, the "A" (Advanced) level exams, were taken by some, usually at age 18. In Scotland, the counterpart to the GCE was the Scottish Certificate of Education (SCE).

In 1973 proposals were put forward for a complete reform of sixth-form exams and curricula. A new Certificate of Extended Education (CEE) was brought in over the 1970s for some of those staying only one year in the sixth.

An increasing number of young people were leaving school with formal qualifications. Only about one-third of school leavers had had such qualifications in the early 1960s. This was up to 80% by the end of the Seventies.

Comprehensives
The move from the mid-1960s was for more comprehensive schools. At the start of the 1970s only about 76% of secondary pupils were in comprehensives. By the end of the decade the figure was 86%. The growth of comprehensives varied from area to area in Britain. In Wales and Scotland the proportion of pupils in comprehensives was over 90%.

Middle Schools
Fifteen Middle Schools, for ages 8 or 9 to ages 12 or 13, opened in 1969. By 1973 there were over 500, and over 1,100 by 1976. Only about 10% of children in this age range were in such schools. These were just one of many educational experiments taking place over the decade.

Countesthorpe
A new school which opened at the start of the Seventies was Countesthorpe, in Leicestershire. It was called "that progressive school", with open-plan buildings. The headmaster and teachers had less "authority" than usual. Children were even calling teachers by their Christian names.

Pupils were free to plan their own work and

34 The new Pimlico school opened in London in 1971. Translucent, expanded PVC foam was set between slices of glass to form the roof. Glass was used freely inside the school as well.

"do their own thing". This meant they also had the freedom to skyve, a problem the school was trying to resolve. On the whole, children seemed to welcome experiments with a freer kind of environment. As one first-year remarked in 1971, "Here there are real nice teachers and you can eat in class."

Free schools
In the early 1970s especially, experiments with "free schools" offered a much less formal education to some children. These were often children having difficulties in more conventional schools. The White Lion Free School opened in London in 1972. By 1974 it had eight permanent staff and 45 children between ages 3 and 15. All the children were expected to do some basic work, but much related to projects which children chose for themselves. Children generally were given much more say in what they would do and how the school was run.

35 The new George Green's Centre in East London, 1976. The Centre was built to include a secondary school, an adult education institute, a youth centre, a sports and leisure centre, a day centre for the elderly and a day nursery. The school had several features not built into previous ILEA schools – for example, a dark room, and a library resources area equipped with a sound-recording studio.

Summer experiment
A revolutionary experiment in 1972 involved schoolboys from Leicestershire, Monmouthshire and Northumberland – and Balliol College, Oxford. Headmasters sent boys who had the ability to do well academically, but who lacked the motivation to go to university. The boys spent three weeks during the summer at Oxford. The idea was to encourage them to try for university places.

Violence, theft and arson
The National Association of Schoolmasters/ Union of Women Teachers began a campaign in the early 1970s to reveal the extent of pupil violence. Attacks on teachers were becoming more and more common. Unruliness in schools seemed to be growing.

More teachers were choosing early retirement, partly because of growing classroom stress. The number of teachers retiring early *quadrupled* between 1969 and 1980.

There was also an increase in thefts from schools and in suspected arson. Police announced in 1975 that they were installing electronic equipment in the schools of two counties to try to curb crime.

Caning
The organization STOPP advised parents in 1976 to threaten legal action against schools using corporal punishment. In 1979, ILEA was among the authorities that banned caning. However, a National Opinion Poll found then an *increasing* number of teachers in *support* of corporal punishment. Growing unrest in schools was a widespread worry.

Anood Shah (b. 1964), who lived in Harrow, remembers "the slipper" as a form of punishment at his school. This was actually a plimsoll whacked against pupils' bottoms.

Resource centres
A trend in the early 1970s was for "resource centres" within schools. These housed collections of materials including newspaper

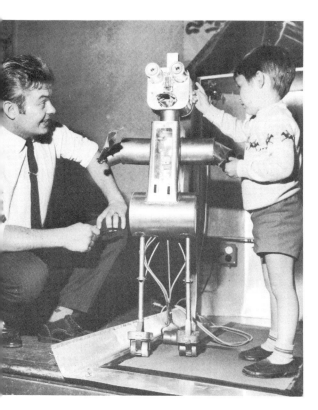

36 A Sunday School teacher in 1971 created a robot to attract children to religious lessons. In the mouth was a loud-speaker giving pre-recorded messages. By the Seventies, attendance at churches was down to about 3% of the population.

clippings, duplicated sheets, tapes and slides. The trend was away from a class being "instructed" and towards group discussion and individual project work. By 1974, resource centres were the "in" thing in schools.

Environmental and Development Education

Environmental Education expanded greatly in schools. The concern was not only about conservation of the countryside but about urban problems as well. Many children found themselves being taken on "town trails", exploring their city or town in a new way. A national WATCH environmental club was set up in 1973, one of many such schemes. Thousands of children took part in surveys of air and water pollution, studying noise and the destruction of wildlife.

Another area which expanded in the 1970s was Development Education. Many more children were learning about world problems and issues, such as the world's rapidly growing population.

Multi-cultural Education

Awareness rose over the Seventies that schools needed to include more in the curriculum both about and for ethnic minorities in Britain. Tulse Hill, in South London, was one school that made quite dramatic changes. Black parents and pupils had voiced their dissatisfaction. In 1973, the Inner London Education Authority (ILEA) arranged a weekend discussion for parents, sixth-formers, staff, ILEA officials, community workers and police. This marked a turning-point for the school. By 1977, courses at Tulse Hill had been changed radically.

37 Britain's first Japanese school opened at Rudgwick, Sussex, in 1972. Many ethnic minority communities were starting Saturday schools and after-school sessions to teach their children who had been born in Britain such "mother tongue" languages as Urdu, Punjabi and Cantonese.

The 1976 Race Relations Act required local education authorities to see that children are not discriminated against. This encouraged help for minorities and more efforts to include learning about the cultures of minorities in the curriculum for *all* pupils.

In 1978, an infants' school in South London put together *The Deptford Cookbook*. There were children from nearly a dozen different cultures in the school. *Aloo Baji* (a vegetable side-dish from Bangladesh) and West Indian Coconut Bread were among the dishes enjoyed by children and included in the book.

Cuts and closures

Spending cuts made it harder for schools to keep up with all the repairs and materials needed. Many children in rural areas also had to travel further to school. At least 500 rural schools closed over the years 1967-77, at the rate of one a week. Pupils joined with parents and teachers in some campaigns to save schools.

In 1971 the Secretary of State for Education was Margaret Thatcher. Her decision to stop free school milk for children aged 7-11 prompted protest at "Thatcher the Milk Snatcher". Some London boroughs defied the ruling.

Computing in schools

There were only about 3,000 computers *in the whole world* in 1960. By 1970, the number was over 75,000. Computers were already being used for many purposes – from traffic control to the drawing of maps from survey data. Very few UK schools had their own computer in 1970. The cost then of buying a new computer for a school or group of schools was £10,000 – £30,000.

There were moves towards teaching computing in UK schools in the 1960s. Scotland was one of the leading areas. A 1969 Scottish curriculum paper recommended that Computer Studies should be provided for most secondary pupils. By the end of 1971, Scotland had set up four regional educational computer

centres based at colleges of education, as well as two more in teachers' centres.

Those who used the centres then in Scotland were mainly maths teachers giving courses in computer programming. Schools sent work to a centre where it was prepared for the computer and processed. The results were then returned to the schools. Pupils usually had to wait a full week before they could see the results of the work they had done.

Small computers became available in the early 1970s, as technology improved. Aberdeen College of Education bought one in 1973. The machine was small enough to be put in a car and taken around from school to school. Pupils were excited at being able to see the computer working, and they could have

38 (1971) Nine- and ten-year-olds had their own school bank to help them save money. Funds were deposited and withdrawn from a real bank nearby. Running the bank gave the pupils practice with maths. By 1985 pocket calculators and computers were described by the Department of Education and Science as "essential" for schools – but in the 1970s, there was still debate over whether these should be used.

immediate results. Other local authorities in Scotland took up the idea. By 1974 there were 14 mobile mini-computers being transported around to schools. No school had the use of the computer for more than one or two weeks in a year.

Scotland's regional centres continued building up facilities. New computers arrived in 1975. However, by 1978 there was still no separate examinable course in computer studies in Scotland.

Meanwhile, no overall policy for schools' computing existed in the rest of Britain. A study began in 1977 to establish a national policy in England and Wales. However, the situation was uneven. *Some* areas in England and Wales were already very active. In other areas, hardly any changes were taking place.

"Batch processing" and "Teleprocessing"

"Batch processing" was the earliest way in which schools in the Seventies had access to a computer. Pupils prepared their programs and data. This was sent to a computer centre where the work was run and the results were returned to the school. In 1973 North Staffs Polytechnic operated a scheme using "mark sensed cards". Pupils prepared programs by marking little boxes on special cards to indicate letters and numbers. These were collected by a van which travelled round to the schools. Programs were run at the centre and the results sent back to schools the next day.

A newer way in which schools had access to a computer was "teleprocessing". Schools had a remote terminal, which was usually a teletypewriter. The GPO installed an extension to a school's existing telephone and connected the "modem" – a device needed to transmit computer information over the 'phone. Sometimes "interactive" communication with a computer was used, providing immediate response via the telephone line.

By 1973, altogether some 300-400 schools across the country were using computer terminals. Many of these schools were in big

39 A flexo-writer machine was used at the Royal Liberty Grammar School in Romford, Essex, in the late 1960s. This was, in fact, the very first school in Britain – and indeed in *Europe* – to have its own computer (in 1965). The school raised the £13,000 needed to buy what was, in 1965, one of the most compact models available. It was 4 feet (1.2m) wide, 3 feet (0.9m) high and 2 feet (0.6m) deep. Several other local schools were allowed to use the computer as well.

cities or near institutions like universities which made facilities available. Nearly 90% of educational computing power was still located in universities.

Terminals used in schools were described in a 1973 *Where* magazine as "no bigger than a pupil's desk but very noisy so in most cases not installed in an actual classroom". Teachers often had pupils prepare their programs on punched paper tape when the terminal was *not* connected to the computer. This saved expensive computer time. When the terminal *was* connected, the tape carrying the program could be "read" quickly.

By 1978, three-quarters of London schools were equipped with terminals and the proportion was similar in Birmingham.

Tavistock School, Devon

Changes at Tavistock School in Devon were an example of what was happening generally over the decade. In 1971, the first move was made to introduce some computer activity. The school joined the Imperial College Schools Computing Scheme. Tavistock paid £15 to cover the cost of a box of cards and three Port-a-Punch sets and access by post to a large computer in London. Over 600 pupils learnt the coding to punch relevant information on to the cards. This was an example of access to a computer by "batch processing".

In 1972, Tavistock won a competition and an on-line terminal was installed at the school with £1,000-worth of time-shared computing. Programs were punched and edited, off-line during the day, and a rota of operators went on-line for one hour each evening. This was an example of "teleprocessing".

In 1973-74 Tavistock introduced computing as a curriculum subject. First-year and sixth-year pupils were given a "computer appreciation" course. Computer studies at "O" level was made available to fourth- and fifth-year pupils. There were programming courses in computer languages BASIC and FORTRAN. In 1974 the school formally established a Computing department.

Computers in schools

Some schools moved in the Seventies from having only a terminal to having a computer of their own. By 1973 the price of a new computer for schools was down to about £3,000. Some

40 In 1979 Moons Moat First School in Redditch, Worcestershire, was just starting to introduce primary children to computers, with a single machine. Headmistress Lillian Simmons has been a pioneer in developing software and using machines with even nursery-aged children. "They learned rapidly to work through a program. We noted an increase in motivation amongst most pupils, and especially those considered 'slower learners'." (By 1985, the school was well into the computer age – with nine micros and two word processors.)

schools bought second-hand equipment dating from the 1960s.

Jane Elton (b. 1964), living near Southampton, was introduced to computers in 1977. "The school had one and it used punch cards. Nothing like the computers now."

By 1978 the new microcomputer was just being launched, small enough to fit on a single desk-top. As the price kept falling, more and more schools were buying. However, by the end of 1980 there were still only about 1,000 computers in UK schools – and many had been bought that year.

Computers and exams

Formal examination courses using computers developed over the 1970s. The demand increased rapidly. There were under 2,000 candidates for CSE and "O" level computing in 1973 – but this was up to over 21,400 by 1977. Nearly 2,000 candidates were presented for "A" level computer studies in 1977.

CAL and CML

Computers were being used also as a learning resource. In some cases the computer presented frames of information and questions. Or the computer contained a model or simulation of an event or environment that learners could manipulate and explore. If some or all of the teaching material was stored *inside* the computer, or if the computer acted as a tool for the learner, this was called computer-assisted learning (CAL).

In 1974, a catalogue of thirty CAL packages covered the following subject areas: ecology, chemistry, computing, economics, environmental studies, geography, history, home economics and physics. Computing was gradually being used for much more than just maths.

If the teaching material was stored *outside* the computer, the term computer-managed learning (CML) was used. Computers were helping to manage learning by marking tests and processing examination results. Computers also suggested materials to be used, based on how well pupils were performing.

One important computer-managed learning project began in Havering, Essex, in 1970. The system devised used the computer to select for individual students a series of work tasks called CALTS (computer-aided learning tasks). The selection was made based on stored information about the students' abilities. Completed work was sent to the computer which analysed results and selected appropriate next tasks.

Projects and materials

An increasing amount of computer-based materials for learning became available over the decade. The government-funded, five-year National Development Programme in Computer-Assisted Learning began in 1973. This supported projects all over the country. The Schools Council project, "Computers in the Curriculum" also started in 1973. Their initial emphasis was on geography, history and economics as well as natural sciences. In 1974, the materials produced by Computer Education in Schools (CES) were in use in over 1,100 schools.

Computers and primary schools

In the mid-1970s, there was still very little activity with computers in UK primary schools. In 1975 Glasgow began using ten terminals in each of ten primary schools, for computer-assisted learning in maths and reading. Another use of the computer for primary schools, involving LOGO, was just starting in the UK. LOGO is a child's programming language to be used in an open way to solve problems.

Computers and administration

Computers were also being used increasingly behind the scenes in education. It was 1970 when the first UK schools tried a computer-based system for timetabling. Other programs became used for such tasks as arranging course options and exams.

8 Books and Magazines

Favourite books

Children's reading in the years 1969-74 was surveyed by the Schools Council. Enid Blyton was top of the list of favourite authors for children aged 10, 12 and 14. Charles Dickens was in second place. Jane Elton (b. 1964), living near Southampton, recalls Enid Blyton as a firm first choice. "In the same vein, with the mystery and the suspense, you used to progress into Agatha Christie. I began with her books when I was about 10."

For the Schools Council survey, children were asked to name the books they read voluntarily in March 1971. An "extraordinary diversity" of titles were mentioned – from *Sam Pig Goes to Market* (Alison Uttley) to *Women in Love* (D.H. Lawrence). For 10-year-olds, the most commonly named books were *Black Beauty*, followed by *Treasure Island* and *The Secret Seven*. Twelve-year-olds most often named *Little Women, Black Beauty* and *Treasure Island*. Fourteen-year-olds most commonly named *Little Women*, followed by *Skinhead* (Richard Allen) and *The Day of the Triffids* (John Wyndham). The report noted a "disturbing trend" away from voluntary reading as children moved from age 10 to 14. Girls of all ages reported reading more books than boys.

New books

The number of new books for children was increasing over the 1970s. Over 3,000 were published in 1979 alone. *Watership Down* came out in 1972 and was one of the decade's most famous. Two especially popular picture books published for young children in the late 1970s were *Mr. and Mrs. Pig's Evening Out* and *John Brown Rose and the Midnight Cat*. There was a huge increase in the sales of children's paperbacks. Puffin more than doubled their sales over the Seventies.

Children's book groups developed all over the country during the decade. These were associations of parents wanting to choose the best of the new books for their children.

Despite the wealth of new stories, it was still the old ones that many children liked best. Sonya Wilson (b. 1968), living in London, used to like fairy tales. "My mum used to read me fairy tales at night. I liked the Princess and the Pauper, Jack and the Beanstalk."

Book clubs and bookshops

The Puffin Club for children started in the late 1960s and grew over the 1970s. Other book clubs for children were popular as well. Bookworm, a children's paperback book club, expanded in 1978 to include choices for 5-7-year-olds.

More bookshops especially for children opened in the decade. The School Bookshop Association, promoting the sale of books in schools, was started in 1976. A poll by the association in 1978 found that over half a million pounds was being spent in the 5,000 school bookshops then operating. Over 40% of those bookshops had been started since 1976. Most books sold were paperbacks.

Magazines and comics

Some favourite magazines and comics continued right through the decade and into the 1980s. Examples were *The Beano* (started

1938), *The Dandy* (started 1937), *Hotspur* (started 1933), *Judy* (started 1960), *Mandy* (started 1967) and *Topper* (started 1953).

Many new titles appeared, too. *Blue Jeans* began in 1977, a colour magazine aimed at teenage girls, with photo love stories, pop music features and pin-ups of pop stars. *Debbie*, also aimed at female readers, first came out in 1973. *Warlord* appeared in 1974, with war picture stories aimed at boy readers.

Very young children had their magazines as well. *Twinkle* (started 1968) was a favourite with Heather McNeil (b. 1965), living near Glasgow: "I liked the stories about Nurse Nancy and her dolls' hospital." *Little Star* appeared from 1972-6 and *Magic* from 1976-9.

The 1970s was the last time that some old children's favourites were seen. For example, *Rover* (a boys' magazine begun in 1922) was last published in 1973.

Magazines related to pop music were increasingly popular from the late 1970s. Jane Elton (b. 1964), living near Southampton, remembers *Smash Hits* starting up in 1977. "I thought it was a good magazine but you could only buy it once every so often. The magazines were expensive for people who were at school. One person used to buy it one week and we all used to read it. Someone else would buy it the next week. But if there was an article you wanted for your wall you had to buy it yourself really."

Magazines were a regular source of decoration for bedrooms. Jane Elton: "I smothered my walls with pictures. My friends did as well. Pop stars, anything."

41 A six-year-old listened to a bedtime story. A new Post Office service of "Dial-a-Story" began in 1971. This was just part of expanding telephone services over the 1970s. It became possible in 1970 to dial directly across the Atlantic for the first time, without going through the operator.

9 Entertainments, Holidays and Leisure

Television

By the 1970s, 96% of all homes in Britain had at least one television. Children aged 5-15 were watching more than anyone else, and more than their age-group had watched in the 1960s. The average by 1978 was about 24 hours' viewing a week by children, girls watching somewhat less than boys.

Young people were also much more likely to be watching a *colour* television in the Seventies than in the Sixties. The number of colour television licences was only 75,000 in 1968 but rose dramatically to nearly 12 million by 1978.

In 1977 Britain saw its first breakfast TV, on Yorkshire Television.

TV for children

The number of programmes especially for children continued to rise. Several favourites, such as *Blue Peter* (which had begun in 1958) and *Magpie* (which had started in 1968), continued to be popular. There were also some television "firsts" for children. For example, *John Craven's Newsround*, the first regular television news programme for children, began in 1972.

42 In 1970 television's *Blue Peter* launched an appeal for forks and spoons. These were used to buy holiday caravans for the thousands of children not able to go on holiday. School-children helped with the sorting.

A serial called *Grange Hill* was started in 1978. Set in a comprehensive school, *Grange Hill* was condemned by some adults for its bad language and rowdyism. Many parents and teachers objected to the way it featured truancy, petty thieving, sit-ins, bullying and smoking. However, *Grange Hill* was a firm favourite with young people. The writer explained: "*Grange Hill* is the first time children have been given their own dramatic series dealing with their world and their problems, where children behave as children do – not how adults think they do."

Another new series for children in the 1970s was *Jim'll Fix It*, hosted by Jimmy Saville. This began in 1975, giving young people the chance to fulfil dreams and wishes – from singing with a pop star to visiting Sri Lanka to see how tea is grown.

TV: effects on children

There were increasing worries over the 1970s about the effects of television on children. Besides serials about police and criminals, there was the real-world violence being shown in news reports. Heather McNeil (b. 1966), living near Glasgow: "On the news there were always pictures of wars. I kept asking why they were fighting." In 1977 the National Viewers' and Listeners' Association blamed television violence for the breakdown of discipline in schools.

TV expands

Over the decade, television became much more than just a box showing pictures. The first teletext information service, "Ceefax", was started by the BBC in 1974. Teletext was only a £100,000 market in 1976. By the end of the Seventies, this had become a £100-million-a-year market.

Video cassette recorders also expanded the use of television. A video tape recorder had been developed as far back as 1956 for the use of broadcasters. It was in 1973 that the first video cassette recorder for television viewers went on sale to the public.

43 Prestel services were begun by the Post Office in 1979. Viewers with special television sets can press buttons on a small key pad to call up information on the screen. By the end of the Seventies, there were already 150 organizations providing over 180,000 pages of Prestel data, constantly updated. Prestel uses the telephone line to link a user's TV set to a computer. Prestel means more than just receiving information on the screen. It is two-way. Ideas being developed will allow viewers to order goods displayed on the screen and send messages to other Prestel sets.

In 1977 a "second generation" of recorders became available, with much better-quality recording. What had been only a £10-million market in 1976 was a £165-million market by the end of the decade.

Cinemas, shows and exhibitions

As television-watching increased over the 1970s, going to the cinema was less popular. There were over 237 million admissions to films in 1968 – but this was down to 125 million by 1978. Many British cinemas were being converted to "three-in-ones". There were, however, some very popular films in the decade.

The 1970 film of *Kes* used the acting talents of North Country children to tell the story of a young boy and a kestrel. *The Tales of Beatrix Potter* in 1971 used famous dancers to dramatize the animal stories. More sinister was *The Clockwork Orange* in 1971, about teenage vandals of the future. *Star Wars* was first shown in 1977 and the animated film version of *Watership Down* was released in 1979.

An extra "AA" category was added by the Board of Film Censors in 1970. "AA" meant that the film was suitable for those over age 14. As films became bolder, the "X" certificate changed its meaning in 1971. Before, unaccompanied young people over age 16 were allowed to see an "X" film. Now the age minimum was *18* years.

There were several musical shows with special appeal for the young. The musicals *Jesus Christ Superstar* and *Godspell* both began in London in 1972. *Hair*, which had begun in the late 1960s, continued to play to full houses.

New theatres and exhibition centres opened – including the National Exhibition Centre in Birmingham and the National Theatre complex on London's South Bank. Many children were at the British Museum in 1972 to see the Tutankhamun Exhibition (with treasures from the ancient Egyptian tomb).

Radio and cassettes

Young people listening to the radio in 1970 could choose between the BBC or offshore "pirate" stations. Commercial radio stations were just starting. The BBC was experimenting with the idea of local radio, and Radio London began in October that year.

Cassettes were increasingly popular over the decade. Car radio/cassette players first became available in the UK in 1972. In 1979 the Walkman boogie-pak was launched in Japan. Within a year this was being sold in Britain. The craze developed for listening to music through personal headphones while on the street.

Youth organizations

Membership of many UK organizations for young people grew. Scouts and Girl Guides together had over a million members by the end of the decade. A survey of 13-16-year-olds

44 An ex-London Transport double-decker bus became a toddlers' club for under-fives in 1972. The play-bus was well-equipped with toys, dolls, a Wendy House, climbing frame and sand and water trays. The conductor bell was kept working, and happily pulled by the children.

showed about 40% belonging to some youth organization.

Scott Thomas (b. 1968), living in South Wales, was at a local church youth club in the late Seventies, "mostly playing ping pong and darts". They used to go on trips to play nearby teams and then have a meal and disco at the other club.

Playgroups and activities

Over the 1970s government aid to playgroups increased. With more mothers working, there was a growing need to supervise children safely. Play schemes of all kinds developed, including adventure playgrounds and summer play activities. In 1971 in Walworth, South London, mothers and children aged 4-14 helped clear a site. 140 children each paid 5p a week to use the adventure playground, watched by two play-leaders.

During the summer holidays in 1974 there were over 80 Inner London Education

45 (1974) The first "Kidsplay" was held in the summer of 1973 at the Tate Gallery in London. Sessions included experiences with textures and colours, as well as visual games. Youngsters could even look through tiny windows at an "upside-down room". At Kidsplay II, in summer 1974, there were sessions to help young people enjoy famous works of art. Children filled in pieces of a giant jigsaw of a well-known painting.

Authority play centres based in primary schools. Children came to play games, make things, draw, act and paint. Light meals were provided. The school bus service helped with taking children out to places of interest.

Museums provided more activities for young people. In 1971 children released 90 racing pigeons from the Tate Gallery, to celebrate Picasso's 90th birthday. Each child received a special folder with Picasso's painting *Girl Holding Pigeon* on the front. At the London Museum in the summer of 1972, children were taught how to make brass rubbings and rubbings from patterns like coal holes in the street.

Holidays

Many more children were able to go on a holiday in the 1970s than in the 1950s. And the number of people going *abroad* was four times as many in 1979 as it had been in 1950.

Children of the Seventies also found that their parents had more holiday time. In 1960 few manual workers had more than two weeks' holiday a year. By the end of the 1970s, one third of these workers had four weeks off or more.

Camping and caravanning were used by 5% of holiday-makers in the 1950s. This rose to 25% of holiday-makers by the end of the Seventies. Heather McNeil (b. 1965), living near Glasgow: "We used to go on camping holidays all the time, touring the Highlands in a van. We stayed in youth hostels as well."

46   A "Treasure Island" play centre opened at Eastbourne in 1973. Fibre-glass models included such figures as crocodiles, a lion, a hippo, a spouting whale and a Zulu in a canoe (shown in the photo). Other attractions included paddling pools, refreshments and climbing ropes.

10 Fashion and Music

Early 1970s' fashion

The "mini" skirt was a sensation of the late 1960s. This continued into the early 1970s, but by 1970 the mid-calf "midi" skirt was being worn as well. A fashionable outfit for little and big girls in 1970 was a midi-coat worn with a matching mini-skirt. Very short "hot pants" were a sizzling item of 1971.

Platform shoes and boots, with enormous heels and very thick soles were another major fashion of 1971/72. Sonya Wilson (b. 1968), living in London, remembers trying on what she called her mother's "big cloggers". Her mother shouted at her to take them off. "You'll break your neck," she said to Sonya.

Anood Shah (b. 1964) recalls long, wide, flared trousers, a popular Seventies' fashion, worn by his older sisters. He used to call them "floor sweepers".

Children's clothes

By the end of the 1960s, a children's clothes

47 (1971) Carnaby Street in London, focus of the "Swinging Sixties" decade, began providing trendy clothes for younger children. The shop "Kids in Gear" was selling grown-up styles in mini-sizes for ages 2-10. Teenage fashion-consciousness spread to a much younger age group over the 1970s.

◄ 48 (1974) Romantic long dresses were part of a nostalgic trend. There was much looking back to earlier decades, and even earlier centuries. Young girls enjoyed wearing Kate Greenaway-style dresses for best.

manufacturer was saying: "The past ten years have seen a revolution in children's wear. While quality, value and fit remain as important as ever, the emphasis is on style. New materials and production facilities and higher living conditions have provided designers with undreamed-of opportunities".

It was increasingly true over the Seventies that clothes were designed to please children. In the 1960s the teenager was the focus of young fashion. By the 1970s, eight- to ten-year-olds were also making the decisions. Unlike in earlier generations, children from the age of five had a considerable say in what they wore.

Children of the Seventies were wanting bright colours and more frequent changes of clothes. After about age four, many no longer wanted conventional party clothes of suits and dresses. Special occasions often meant super-jeans and super-T-shirts.

Not all parents agreed with young people wanting to dress in a more free and easy way. Gary Hollander-Woods (b. 1961): "Your parents were always wanting you to dress up a

49 (1976) One of the most important fashion ► trends of the 1970s, for children as well as adults, was denim. Over 44 million pairs of jeans were bought in the UK in 1978. 40% of the UK population bought at least one pair. Denim was made into skirts, waistcoats – just about everything imaginable. One writer wrote: "Denim is more than a fashion. It's practically an extension of our skin." Andy Alexander (b. 1960) remembers really tight jeans with flared trouser legs: "You had to have an iron line. It used to take me two hours to iron a pair of jeans. They had to be perfect."

bit for going out, while everyone was being more casual."

Shops responded to all the changes. Since 1975 there has been a separate children's-wear section at Marks and Spencer. They found that "fashion" was becoming more and more important in children's clothes. British Home Stores used to run similar styles for an age range of 2-13 years. By the mid-1970s they were sub-dividing the range. The idea of having just one new collection of clothes a year changed as well. Children's fashions began to alter more rapidly, making the life of a fashion line just weeks or six months at the most. There was a much increased demand for casual separates, following the adult trend.

A standard best-seller for babies continued to be the "Babygro" or "Babystretch" suit. The idea for one-piece stretch suits for infants began in America in the 1950s. By the 1970s, even Babygro had a new fashion range twice a year.

School uniforms

School uniforms became more relaxed over the decade. The main call was for grey shorts and pullovers, navy blazers, skirts and pinafores, duffle coats and raincoats, white shirts and blouses. The school cap for boys had virtually disappeared. Some girls' boarding schools re-introduced straw boater hats, in navy blue or green, and long capes. Many schools began not to require sixth-form girls to wear uniforms, and some even allowed trousers and jeans to be worn. Older boys' uniforms were still largely grey flannel suits and blazers.

Early 1970s' music

The Beatles, the biggest pop-group phenomenon of the 1960s, officially broke up in the early 1970s. Their music continued to be popular as many other groups appeared. An American singing family, The Osmonds, made their first British appearance in 1972.

Interest in pop stars involved far more than just buying their records. When the Osmonds

50   In 1976 the Weltons, a pop group all under age 15, won the television talent show *Opportunity Knocks*. Their first record was called "Paint Your Sun a Little Brighter".

51 Fans screamed for the Bay City Rollers, a group from Scotland, 1975. Pop music was an important part of the lives of young people in the 1970s. A survey in 1976 showed that 95% of girls in Britain aged 12-18 had a record player at home. Over the year they bought over 15 million single records and 5 million long-playing records.

Top 5 best-selling single records of the year (reprinted courtesy of *Music Week*)

1971
1. MY SWEET LORD (George Harrison)
2. MAGGIE MAY (Rod Stewart)
3. CHIRPY CHIRPY CHEEP CHEEP (Middle of the Road))
4. KNOCK THREE TIMES (Dawn)
5. HOT LOVE (T.Rex)

1975
1. BYE BYE BABY (Bay City Rollers)
2. SAILING (Rod Stewart)
3. CAN'T GIVE YOU ANYTHING BUT LOVE (Stylistics)
4. WHISPERING GRASS (Windsor Davies/Don Estelle)
5. STAND BY YOUR MAN (Tammy Wynette)

1979
1. BRIGHT EYES (Art Garfunkel)
2. HEART OF GLASS (Blondie)
3. WE DON'T TALK ANY MORE (Cliff Richard)
4. I DON'T LIKE MONDAYS (Boomtown Rats)
5. WHEN YOU'RE IN LOVE (Dr. Hook)

visited Britain in 1973 there was a rush to buy Donny caps, tote bags, T-shirts, song books, key rings, stationery. . .

Sonya Wilson (b. 1968) remembers a Scottish group, the Bay City Rollers, who became very popular in 1975: "I was at primary school but the big girls were singing B-A-Y, B-A-Y. We used to sing it like the big people. Everywhere you'd see the Scottish plaid. There were socks, scarves – even a board game that was a little like 'Monopoly'."

55

"Punk" music and fashion

"Punk" music and clothes arrived just after the mid-1970s. Jane Elton (b. 1964), living near Southampton, was in her early teens at the time. "I liked the Bay City Rollers and then suddenly this punk thing came along and I thought, fancy liking *weedy* groups like that. The Rollers just looked so *weedy*." Jane's mum said she "changed overnight". When her parents went to school open day in 1977 they discovered that at school Jane was wearing green hair. Jane explained: "You still had to wear the school uniform so it was all attached to that. Besides the food colouring in our hair, we had lots of safety pins, anywhere. And you used to add zips all over your jeans. Punk was really against the fashion of the time. Flared trousers were still 'in'. Punk was all narrow drain pipe trousers, zips and spikey, different coloured hair. Some people had pink, yellow. . ."

Sonya Wilson (b. 1968) was only nine when

52 Punk rockers, 1978. Safety pins all over was one "in" punk fashion.

she saw a punk with bright orange hair. "I thought, 'How could anyone have hair like that?' I didn't think about dye and all that kind of stuff."

Punk music and fashion definitely marked the start of something different. Jane Elton: "I thought music in the Seventies up to 1976 was very boring. It was all pretty middle-of-the-road stuff. Then came all the electronic sounds, the synthesizers. It was a whole new style of music. Towards the end of the 1970s I used to like groups like Siouxie and the Banshees. And there was the Sex Pistols. They were *notorious*. Gary Glitter started in the early 1970s. I've always liked him. . ."

Andy Alexander (b. 1960) was never interested in punk. "It was smart clothes, Italian pointed shoes, down the disco, chatting up the girls."

53 Fourteen young dancers were chosen as finalists in the 1979 EMI UK Disco Dancing Championship. The first World Disco Dancing Championship was held in London in 1978. Disco dancing became popular in the late 1970s, especially after the film *Saturday Night Fever*.

Conflict with adults

Music, clothes and hairstyles were a source of conflict between teenagers and their parents and teachers over the decade. Andy Alexander (b. 1960): "When earrings came in, you used to wear earrings to school and the teachers would scream at you and tell you to go home." In 1977 girls at a Norfolk school protested against an attempt to ban maxi-skirts and striped socks. In 1979 one boy was suspended for wearing a skirt(!) to school in protest against the banning of girls in trousers.

11 Toys, Games and Sports

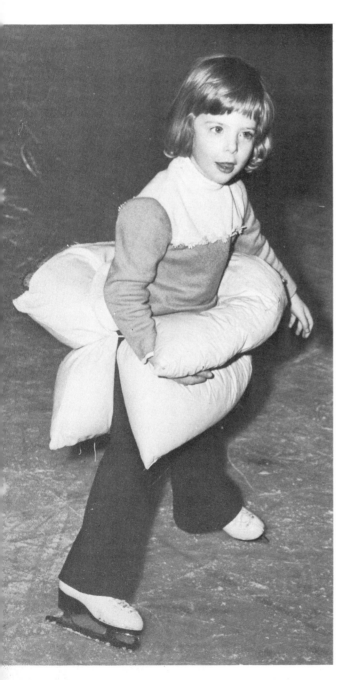

Outdoor games

Many familiar games and sports continued in the 1970s. For Scott Thomas (b. 1968), living in South Wales, rugby was the favourite. "Occasionally you used to play football if you weren't that good at rugby." Gary Hollander-Woods (b. 1961), living in Lincolnshire, (and many others) liked racket games, such as tennis and badminton.

A favourite pastime of mainly girls involved intricate patterns of hand-clapping, underarm and overarm. Usually two facing girls clapped each other's hands, singing chants to match the pattern of claps. Popular 1970s' chants included "Who stole the cookie from the baker's shop?" and "A sailor went to sea, sea, sea. . .". Sonya Wilson (b. 1968), living in London, remembers clapping with her friends to:

> "I went to the Chinese restaurant to buy a loaf of bread, bread, bread. They wrapped it up in a five pound note and this is what they said, said, said. . ."

Another clapping rhyme began:

> "See see my granny, boom boom, I can not play with you, boom boom, my sister's got the flu, boom boom, since nineteen sixty-two, boom boom. . ."

54 (1972) A four-year-old in London was well-padded for the rink. Heather McNeil (b. 1965), living near Glasgow, was one of many other Seventies' children who enjoyed ice skating.

Debbie Tyldesley (b. 1966), living in Manchester: "We used to stick a tennis ball in a nylon stocking and swing it each side of us against the wall, singing a song." A favourite clapping rhyme was "Popeye the Sailor Man". "We used to collect snails, put them in glass jars and sometimes we raced them. When I moved to Bournemouth and we got big snails, sometimes we'd write names on the shells, like 'Frieda'."

Jane Elton (b. 1964), living near Southampton, remembers sports like netball and rounders for girls. Tag and Kiss Chase were as popular as ever, as was skipping. "You'd have two people holding a long piece of knicker elastic at either end. You'd jump over it and gradually it became higher and higher. Some people would chain together elastic bands."

Looping together elastic bands into long chains was also popular near Glasgow.

Heather McNeil (b. 1965): "We used to jump in and out of the chains. It was called playing 'elastics'." When Heather and her friends skipped, they used rope. Their hopscotch games were called "beds". Chalk was used to draw the numbers on the ground. "We threw an old shoe polish tin or something like that."

Skating, skateboarding and windsurfing

Roller-skating was becoming popular again in

55 The Findus/Wheelies Pancake Race was held at the Wheelies Skate Space in London, 1978. Skateboarders held a frying pan and pancake during the race. Skateboarding was a very popular street sport in 1977/78 and some special parks were built. One T-shirt worn at the time said: "Skateboards Rule OK". Anood Shah (b. 1964) broke an arm skateboarding. There were many injuries like that.

the early 1970s. (Its popularity had waned somewhat in the late 1950s and '60s). The appeal was growing among younger children especially. Skates took on a much more glamorous image than in earlier decades. "Flyer GT", launched in 1973, were skates which looked like racing cars, complete with numbers, stickers and flashes. "Disco skating" became a craze in 1979.

Skateboards appeared in Britain in 1976 and were the big news of 1977, reaching the position of fourth most popular toy. By 1979 the "wizz-kart" was launched, a combination of a skateboard and a go-cart. Also in 1979, sailboarding (or windsurfing) developed in Britain as a new sport.

Bicycles
Like roller skates, another old favourite, the bicycle, took a glamorous turn in styling. The exciting "Chopper" bike, launched in 1970, caused a sensation. Its design was unconventional and adventurous. It was followed by the "Strika" bike in 1976 for five- and six-year-olds. The "Strika" had a motorcycle-style front with rubber mock shock-absorbers and scrambling handlebars with thick rubber grips.

Kites
Kite-flying enjoyed a boom in the mid-1970s. The craze was for new, steerable kites that could be made to perform acrobatics in the air. The "Skite" was introduced in 1975.

Boxed indoor games
Many new board and other games were sold in the 1970s. There were over 470 games on sale in Britain by 1976, and 164 of those had been brought out that year.

Games in 1973 included "Chartbuster", a game in which six players were aspiring pop stars promoting their records. "The London Game" was based on the London Underground system, while the "Great Game of Britain" was based on the British Rail network. Old standard board games like draughts, "Ludo",

"Snakes and Ladders" and "Bingo" continued to be popular. "Scrabble", first launched in 1954, was a top-selling game in 1975. Another standard favourite was "Monopoly", launched as far back as 1935.

Best-selling toys
(compiled by *Toys International* magazine)

November 1971	November 1975	November 1979
1. Action Man	1. Lego Bricks	1. Lego Bricks
2. Airfix Kits	2. Mastermind	2. Scalextric
3. Dinko UFO	3. Sindy Doll	3. Action Man
4. Tonka Toys	4. Airfix Kits	4. Ideal TCR
5. Lego	5. Tiny Tears	5. Sindy Doll
6. Action Girl	6. Matchbox	6. Tiny Tears
7. Subbuteo	7. Pippa	7. Corgi Cars/Monopoly
8. Dinky Models	8. Britains	8. Girl's World/Airfix Kits
9. Matchbox Models	9. Scrabble	9. Electronic Mastermind/ Scrabble
10. Haunted House	10. Action Man	10. Fisher Price Activity Centre/Hornby Railways

---

"Year of the Doll"
Manufacturers talked of 1973 as being the "Year of the Doll". Dolls have always been popular, but it was the small figure *fashion* doll that was selling so well. Of the ten best-selling toys in November that year, five were dolls with a complete range of clothes and accessories. "Action Man" was first sold in the mid-1960s. ("Action Girl" was launched in 1971 but never became as popular.) "Little Big Man" was a 16.5cm-tall doll, new in 1973 for

56 New Spear's Project Cards for children aged ▶ 7-12 began appearing in the shops in 1970. For 5/– (the equivalent of 25p), you could buy a pack of ten laminated cards which gave 10 to 15 projects. These showed how to make things from string, paper, old cotton reels, empty cartons, etc. In the space station pack there were instructions on how to make a moon vehicle. In the photo, two 10-year-olds battle as St George and the Dragon, in costumes they have made.

boys. It was boxed with all the accessories for a specific mission. "Mountain Assault" was one of twelve sets available.

Three other best-selling dolls in 1973 were for girls – "Daisy", "Pippa" and "Sindy". "Sindy", sold since 1964, was the best-selling doll of the 1970s. "Pippa" had just started in 1972 and "Daisy" in 1973. They all came with changing wardrobes, wigs and many other accessories.

New fashion dolls in 1973 included "Disco Girl Dolls", designed to look like "record-playing, boutique-crazy teenagers". Manufacturers said that eight-year-old girls, the prime target for dolls, longed to imitate their teenage sisters rather than their mothers. Ranges of clothes for "Disco Girl Dolls" were even packed in record sleeves.

In contrast to the fashion doll, "First Love", launched in 1976, was a doll with a very realistic baby face. The floppy limbs and head moved like those of a real baby.

Sexism in toys

Sonya Wilson (b. 1968), living in London, used to have "lots and lots of dolls". She also wanted some toys less traditionally "for girls". "My brother had a toy car. I said I wanted a red car and my mother said no, have this dolly instead. She got me marbles but she didn't get me a toy car." The idea of sexism in toys became a talking point in the 1970s. There were moves to encourage a wider range of toys and games for both boys *and* girls.

Figures to be played with by *both* boys and girls were a growing 1970s' focus. "Playpeople" was launched in 1976 for 3-7-year-olds and became the best-selling toy by November that year. The hand-sized 7.5cm-high, plastic figures were virtually indestructible, with

57 (1973) The "Buzzcart" was a tough, fast, steerable vehicle which could be converted quickly into a steerable sledge.

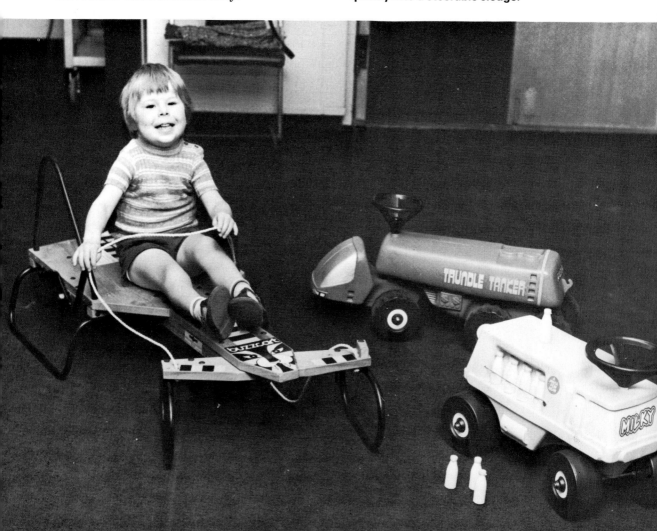

moveable arms, legs, head and waist. Sets of accessories and objects were on separate themes. The first three sets were Knights, Cowboys and Indians, and Builders.

By 1976, the Airfix company had about 400 different model kits on sale. The range included aeroplanes, boats, cars, motorbikes, space travel and military figures. Model-making had always been considered a "boy's hobby" – but that was changing. Some models specifically for girls' interest (e.g. one of Queen Elizabeth I) were introduced.

By 1977, manufacturers were providing more and more alternatives to just dolls for girls. Craft kits with special appeal to girls included tapestry and macrame (knot-tying).

"Characters" of the Seventies

There was a boom in favourite characters in the 1970s, used for everything from toys and books to T-shirts and stationery. Some characters, like Disney's Mickey Mouse, had been around for decades. Tom and Jerry and Rupert Bear were also featured on many products. The fastest-selling characters of 1975 were The Wombles. New favourites in 1976 were Paddington Bear, the Woozles and the Muppets.

The Muppets was an American-produced puppet television series which first appeared on British screens in 1976. The characters of Kermit the Frog, Fozzie Bear and Miss Piggy were seen everywhere. In 1978 *Star Wars* was the theme of many toys, linked to the popular film. A television series, *The Incredible Hulk*, prompted many play items in 1979, including a painting set and game. Another favourite of 1979 were new Mr Men toys, linked to the books for young children.

Electronic games

As early as 1973, *Toys International*, a magazine for those who make and sell toys, noted: "An electronics revolution which could have greater influence on world affairs than the industrial revolution of the 19th century is gathering momentum." In 1977 the first

electronic non-TV game was introduced (Chess). Tank and battle games also came into the shops. A hand-held educational toy for children was launched as well. "The Little Professor" used calculator-design circuitry. When a correct answer was given, the Professor set another problem. When a wrong answer was given, the problem was repeated. After three wrong answers, the right answer appeared.

In 1978 about one million electronic games were sold in Britain. In addition, about 40,000 higher-priced games were sold, based on the micro-computer. The leading micro-computer game was "Grandstand". Customers could choose up to 17 different cartridges, costing about £20 each. There was programming for up to four different games on each cartridge.

In 1979 *Toys International* said: "Electronic games and toys look like becoming the rage." One of the first to become popular that year was "Simon", imported from the USA. This was modelled on a flying saucer, with four coloured lights. Matching buttons had to be pressed to follow a sequence of lights shown. Other electronic chip-based toys available in 1979 included "Merlin", "Demon Driver" and "Muson" (an electronic synthesizer). There was even "Zero-1", a new electronic control system for model trains.

Also launched in 1979 was "Compute-a-tune", the musical computer with a memory. "Dentist" was introduced as "the hilarious electronic game of extracting teeth". "Stop Boris" included a monster spider (Boris) advancing "relentlessly towards a player" until he was stopped and returned to his spider-web home "by the accurate firing of a ray-gun between his glowing eyes."

"Mastermind", the code-breaking game, had started in 1972 and was a best-seller by 1975. In 1979 "Electronic Mastermind" was introduced. This had its own processor and two specially devised printed circuits.

Television and arcade games

Patents for consumer electronic television

games were given as early as 1966. It was 1972 before electronic technology actually made them possible. The first discrete component bat and paddle game was launched that year. It was in the late 1970s that electronic TV games became widely popular. Only about £1.4 million was spent on these in 1976 – compared to £30 million by the end of the decade.

"Space Invaders", an arcade game, arrived in Britain in 1979. There was concern that some young people were spending much time and money on these machines. Andy Alexander (b. 1960): "There was people hooked on it, spending every penny they'd got. Got a bit hooked myself."

Old favourites remain

Despite technological changes, the best-selling toys were still the traditional favourites, even by the end of the decade. Of 1979's 10 best-sellers, the only "new technology" toy was "Electronic Mastermind". One in every three toys bought in 1979 was still a doll or soft toy. Heather McNeil (b. 1965), living near Glasgow, clung to "a small cuddly furry rabbit". A great favourite in 1978 was a gooey green substance called "Slime".

58 In 1972, "do-it-yourself" television arrived in Britain. A new closed-circuit system called "Odyssey" was used to help teach pre-school children numbers and letters. The system could also be used to play remote-controlled games such as table-tennis and hockey. Electronic television games became very popular in the late 1970s.

12 Multi-Ethnic Society

Immigration

Britain has been a great mix of nationalities for thousands of years. Young people of the 1970s had more chances to meet people from other ethnic groups, and more chances to enjoy their cultures. Anood Shah (b. 1964) had an English friend, Paul, who liked the Indian food made by Anood's mother. "He used to love my

59 **(1971) An orphan from the Vietnam War (which ended in 1975) arrived in Britain with 23 others. She was one recent arrival of the immigrants who have been coming to Britain for thousands of years. The variety of skills and cultures brought by immigrants has made Britain a much richer and more interesting place in which to live.**

mother's cooking and watching dishes being prepared."

After the Second World War, Britain was very short of workers and especially *encouraged* immigrants from the New Commonwealth. This included those from colonies in Asia, the West Indies and Africa that became independent in the years after the War.

In the 1960s, Britain began to limit immigration by a series of Commonwealth Immigration Acts. The Act which came into force on 1 January 1973 limited immigration very strictly, mainly to those with needed skills.

60 (1979) A huge party for children, held in Hyde Park, attracted over 160,000. This celebrated the International Year of the Child. There were many other activities throughout Britain, including a marathon by Scottish schools to raise funds.

Refugees

The law has allowed the immigration of close dependents of people already settled in the UK. Also allowed are holders of UK passports who have been driven out of countries in which they have been living. In 1972, the Ugandan President declared he was expelling from the country all Asians with British passports. The

Ugandan Asians who arrived in the UK included many teenagers and children. A Resettlement Board was set up, to help families find homes and jobs.

Another main group of refugees who came to Britain in the 1970s were from Vietnam. In 1979 thousands of expelled, homeless "boat people" were accepted by different countries. Over 5,000 came to Britain.

Children of immigrants

In 1976 there were about 750,000 children under age 16 in Britain who were of New Commonwealth and Pakistani origin. These were about 5% of all children in the UK. Some of these young people were born overseas, but 85% were born in Britain. Anood Shah (b. 1964) was born in Kenya and came to Britain at the age of three. Sonya Wilson (b. 1968) was born in South London. Her parents came from Jamaica in the early 1960s.

There were also many children born in *other* parts of the world, or whose parents had come from other countries.

International Year of the Child

All nationalities in Britain helped celebrate the United Nations' "Year of the Child" in 1979. A UK Association for this included over 600 groups – from charities and youth organizations to community, church and pressure groups. The Association published pamphlets and ran projects like a children's legal centre. There was also fund-raising for children overseas. Events for children in Britain included many local festivals and competitions. The main national events were a children's party in Hyde Park and Young People's Parliaments in London, Coventry and Wales.

The Year, celebrated worldwide, was a fitting end to the decade. The special needs, rights and problems of young people were being noticed increasingly over the Seventies. Andy Alexander (b. 1960): "It was really children speaking up. . ."

Date List

1970   General Election: Conservatives' Edward Heath elected PM.
          Age of majority lowered from 21 to 18 on 1 January.
          First topless newspaper pin-up.
          New-style "Chopper" bicycle launched.

1971   "D-Day", 15 February: decimal coinage introduced.
          First Women's Liberation march in Britain.
          Family Income Supplement started to help poorest families.
          Open University began.

1972   Start of VAT (Value Added Tax) at 8%.
          Contraceptives became available free to all over age 16.
          '72-'73: school-leaving age raised to 16.
          First electronic television game launched.
          World's first pocket calculator on sale.

1973   Britain entered European Economic Community (EEC) on 1 January.
          First video cassette recorder for television on sale to public.
          Commonwealth Immigration Act into force, 1 January.
          Employment of Children Act.

1974   General Election, February: Labour's Harold Wilson elected PM.
          General Election, October: Labour's Harold Wilson re-elected PM.
          Renaming of some counties, change of some borders, effective 1 April.
          Ceefax television information service started by BBC.
          Finer Report on one-parent families.

1975   Margaret Thatcher chosen as first woman leader of Conservatives.
          Britain's first solar-heated house (in Milton Keynes).
          Sex Discrimination Act and Equal Opportunities Commission set up.
          Children's Act.

1976   Nobel Peace Prize to Mrs Betty Williams and Miss Mairead Corrigan for working to end violence in Northern Ireland.
          First commercial North Sea Oil came ashore.
          Passenger services on Concorde, first supersonic airliner, began.
          Drought crisis in summer.
          Race Relations Act.
          Skateboards appeared in Britain.

1977   VAT raised to 15%.
          Queen's Silver Jubilee marking 25 years of her reign.
          First non-TV electronic game introduced in UK.

1978   "Youth Opportunities Programme" launched.
          World's first test-tube baby born in Oldham, England.
          First World Disco Dancing Championship, in London.

1979   General Election: Conservatives' Margaret Thatcher elected PM.
          First Euro-MPs elected in Britain, to attend European Parliament.
          Child Benefit payments replaced Family Allowances.
          Prestel television service launched by Post Office.
          International Year of the Child.

1980   First home computer selling for under £100 (Sinclair ZX 80).
          Education Act.

Glossary

age of majority	age at which certain basic rights are granted to young people – eg right to make wills
freezes (pay and prices)	wages and prices held as they are for a set time to help keep down inflation
latch-key children	children left to fend for themselves after school because both parents are working
MORI	Market and Opinion Research International; organization which collects opinion and attitude data about social topics
plebiscite	a direct vote by the whole of the electors to decide a question of public importance
referendum	the act of submitting the direct decision of a question at issue to the whole body of voters
shilling	British coin used until early 1970s when decimal coinage started; equivalent of five new pence; twenty shillings equalled one pound
state of emergency	government declaration of time of extreme crisis in country when special measures are needed to cope
theft/burglary	theft = stealing; burglary = breaking into premises to steal
three-in-one cinema	one large old cinema converted into three smaller ones, each showing a different film
Ulster	another name for the six counties of Northern Ireland

Books for Further Reading

Allison, Ronald, *Britain in the Seventies*, Country Life Books, 1980
Bartlett, C.J., *A History of Post-War Britain 1945-1974*, Longman, 1977
Madjwick, P.J. and others, *Britain Since 1945*, Hutchinson, 1982
Marwick, Arthur, *British Society Since 1945*, Penguin, 1982

The author warmly thanks the following for contributing memories to this book:

Andy Alexander
(b. 1960)

John Alexander
(b. 1958)

Jane Elton
(b. 1964)

Gary Hollander-Woods
(b. 1961)

Heather McNeil
(b. 1965)

Anood Shah
(b. 1964)

Scott Thomas
(b. 1968)

Debbie Tyldesley
(b. 1966)

Sonya Wilson
(b. 1968)

Index

The numbers in **bold type** refer to the figure numbers of the illustrations